Personality Development

Personality Development

Sutapa Banerjee

I.K. International Publishing House Pvt. Ltd.

NEW DELHI • BANGALORE

Published by
I.K. International Publishing House Pvt. Ltd.
S-25, Green Park Extension
Uphaar Cinema Market
New Delhi–110 016 (India)
E-mail : info@ikinternational.com
Website: www.ikbooks.com

ISBN 978-93-81141-84-7

10 9 8 7 6 5 4 3 2 1

Published by Krishan Makhijani for I.K. International Publishing House Pvt. Ltd., S-25, Green Park Extension, Uphaar Cinema Market, New Delhi–110 016 and Printed by Rekha Printers Pvt. Ltd., Okhla Industrial Area, Phase II, New Delhi–110 020.

Preface

This book endeavours to show how the subtle integration of emotions blended with literary thoughts, art and culture enhances the personality of professionals. The expertise that the entrepreneurs and professionals acquire through tenacity, hard work and assiduous cultivation of their inherent talent is given an upward thrust by the development of their personality. A detailed and an elaborate discussion will give us multidimensional perception of the need and essence of personality development in various walks of life that help one achieve career goals.

Each one of us is born with some potential bestowed on us. That can be developed through training and spiritual discipline. Such training and development have profound influence on the personality of an individual to shape his life by enriching his outlook, behavioural pattern and interactive style. The leaders, the managers, the professionals and the entrepreneurs leverage that to optimize human resources in attaining organizational goals.

I have been associated with B schools and engineering colleges as a teacher for a considerable period of time. During my tenure of teaching I observed closely the students. They often exhibit exemplary courage and strength of character. However they may lack in some important skills and elements that shadow their inner strength and character. These seekers of profession will lead an organization later on. Will they be able to execute their tasks with competence I often wondered! My area of teaching is soft skills and personality development. And while performing this role I gradually realized that I need to discuss some very interesting aspects of personality development in the form of a book. This observation allowed me to glean several important facts that I have a conviction, will help in developing the personality of an individual who can reap an advantage by dint of those important areas that comprise a number of acquired attributes. That precisely will help them create an iconic image in their world of profession.

So I have taken this up as a relevant content of my book. And I have conviction that my readers will perceive the necessity of developing personality in multidimensional colours for the collective growth of organization, society and nation. They will also concede the dual need of IQ and EQ to play the pivotal role of a successful person in life. To conclude I need to add that this book is not meant for professionals only but for people belonging to any walk of life.

Author

Acknowledgements

This scribe is entirely based on the observations I have had during my tenure of teaching. I have quoted some authors from books and newspapers where I found my finding and observation sync with theirs. I am grateful to them and I am also grateful to WBUT (West Bengal University of Technology) for offering me to take a class on Personality Development for the B. Tech students. My association with ICFAI Business School, IIPM, Kolkata and Bhavan's Institute of Management Sciencc as faculty member has helped me in gleaning some relevant input for my book.

I am thankful to my colleagues and students for the interactive process we go through pertaining to personality development.

I would like to thank my husband SSB, for being very encouraging and supportive throughout.

Author

Contents

Author

Dr Sutapa Banerjee is an Education maestro with a difference. She has spent the past 25 years in pursuit of excellence in the Queen's language, with equal ramifications in pure and applied English.

The author exhibited a keen interest in English having acquired her ***Bachelor's and Master's Degrees from the prestigious Dept. of English, Jadavpur University, Kolkata.*** In addition, she penned down a debatable yet versatile study of characters in the novels of Emily Bronte and Jane Austen. This not only earned her a ***Ph.D. from Jadavpur University,*** but also won her accolades from her International jury. Keen to realize the depth of our Education System, the author concurrently acquired another Master's Degree in English specializing in American Literature. Later, she also completed a Post Graduation in ***HR Management from ICFAI University,*** in a successful bid to marry up applied English and the unchartered world of Human Resources.

Dr Banerjee's vast teaching experience outdoes her immense educational qualifications. She has successfully and singlehandedly taught students majoring in English literature and students pursuing professional courses like Engineering and MBA! This equips her with an in-depth comprehension of our country's Education and the lacunae therein. Having taught mainstream English, the author followed applied English at Engineering Colleges affiliated to ***West Bengal University of Technology,*** Kolkata. For the past decade she has taught MBA students at B-Schools of repute including ***ICFAI Business School*** and ***IIPM.*** She also heads English Examinations for West Bengal University of Technology and guides the University in Curriculum modernization and redevelopment as a member of the board of studies.

Dr Banerjee realizes that being an IEC node is impossible without reaching out to students across our diverse Geography. In expediting the same, she authored widely acclaimed books on contemporary applied English for development of Soft Skills, including ***English for Engineering and Management, Soft Skills: Business and Professional Communication, English Language and Technical Communication.*** Her journal article (on ***Target Group Profile and Communication***) published in the **ICFAI Journal of Soft Skills** was highly appreciated. She has her contribution in ***Hindustan Times*** as a columnist too.

1

Personality

1. What is personality? Why do we need to develop our personality?

Personality denotes all the attributes that a person is endowed with, that make him/her the person he/she is. The term when considered comprehensively includes some features that are essential components of human beings. That emphasizes both external as well as internal components. And these components in turn are germinated and nurtured either by instinctive and inherent propensities or by social and environmental agents. When we talk about someone having a strong personality we mean generally that he or she is a person who has strong opinions and possesses very firm views, attitudes and perception. Here what is striking is that we do not consider one specific attribute when we talk about personality. Rather we go by a host of attributes to signify and indicate any individual's personality. Personality determines an individual's inclinations, habits, behaviour, interaction and style of communication. There are some other features that may be included as the decisive factors to describe one's personality. Let us explore and see what comprises personality.

Since our childhood we go through various phases in life. The various phases that we talk about can be unique in every individual's case. When considered collectively it is the geographical locations, socio-economic background, gender difference and education that come into the forefront. When considered individually, apart from the above considerations we have some other factors like inherited traits as familial pride and vanity etc. that cannot be overlooked. That has newer dimensions added to the factors mentioned above to develop one's personality. Obviously all these together constitute our personality. So when we refer to someone being very noble we highlight his nobility in respect to his personality that refers to his good and honest principles in life, his fellow feelings and perhaps his honest dealings with everyone around him. Again when we talk about someone as proud we indicate the pride or vanity that affects his gait, communication style, dealing with people and behavioural attitude. Thus we see personality reflects some attributes collectively and it is not like saying someone is *good* or *bad*.

To take some practical examples we can consider two individuals belonging to two different countries: one from India and another from China. The two persons will have different personalities on account of their being from two different nations as there is a marked difference in culture in the two different countries. But both of them may be very good. The culture that directs some of our values pertaining to habits and trends will definitely be different in two individuals hailing from the two countries. As such there will be difference in mindset that is often influenced by the cultural practices of one's nation, community or environment that one belongs to. Hence the difference in their personalities, that will be apparent when it is manifested in behavioural expressions. However both of them can be regarded as smart fellows if they have their look and appearance smart. Here the background may not affect their personalities in regard to look or appearance at all.

This is an example of people belonging to two nations. Again there can be wide difference in personalities between two people though belonging to the same nation, the reason being they have a wide gap in socio-economic background. In educational institutes this can be seen and it is quite tangible at certain levels. In graduate schools at the tertiary level we find difference in socio-economic background affecting the personalities of students quite conspicuously. On one hand there are students who are noted for their smartness, boldness, communication skill and formal etiquette. On the other there are students who suffer from hesitations and diffidence that affect their competence in various activities. The reason is the former belong to a higher socio-economic background and have elite school background whereas the latter come from a less affluent class with ordinary background having attended the schools that have vernacular as their medium of instruction. The question here is not money or wealth. It is the background comprising social milieu in which one is brought up. The outcome is the difference in personality that is reflected in one's interaction. The ones coming from the elite classes feel more confident and at times are found to possess an arrogant attitude towards the fellow students, teachers and the others. Their behaviour sometimes is noted to be impolite and discourteous. Again those who come from places and background where they are not acquainted with the behavioural responses maintaining the protocol of the formal set up feel uneasy and grow inferiority complex. However we cannot generalize on the basis of one or two examples. There may be students in this group who are polite enough and are more particular about their behaviour and courtesies. They may come from an affluent class with good socio-economic background and yet they do not have the negativity that we normally associate with the personality of the ones belonging to an affluent class.

Quite on the contrary the group of students falling in the category of less affluent class and not having attended an English-medium school or used to the formalities of the decorum followed seem to have different kind of personality. Yet they may be smart and quick in adapting to the environmental gap. Though some of them may feel shy and withdrawn that affects their emotional response and ultimately their personality. Here external agents like society influences in the development of their personality. This is an observation that is based on commonly noted instances. However among them too we find students who exhibit outstanding behavioural development in an entirely different ambience. That is the inherent trait of personality that the students have and the adaptability that they imbibe from external sources make them shape their personality with the desired result. Whether one is familiar with the formal etiquette that we observe is immaterial when one is able to pick up from the environment in which one is positioned.

The humility and modesty that we imbibe from our parents and our near ones give us the admirable personality and everybody likes us. In other words these help us, develop ourselves in getting such personality. One only needs to brush up some of the relevant areas of soft skills to increase emotional intelligence that help them to become polite, smart and confident. The ones who are from a more affluent background and some of whom are arrogant and over confident need to tone down and acquire those skills that make them change their attitude. They need to be encouraged to read and perceive situations with a penetrative insight in order to understand the significance of those virtues that one must be endowed with if one wants to have an impressive personality.

EMOTIONAL INTELLIGENCE

In the current age we cannot fail to notice one intimidating element that engulfs us. All of us are vulnerable to excessive stress in this competitive world. Whatever profession we may be in we find the persistent struggle to survive and go ahead, driving us crazy. Many of us are victimized and cannot resist the stress. Few of us can cope up with the stress we are faced with. In order to come out from such a stressful situation what we need is a balanced personality that helps us overcome adverse situations. Personality can be developed by sharpening and developing our soft skills that are complementary to our technical skills. Our personality comprises certain key features and the proper honing of those features helps us to balance our emotions that we need to possess in times of contingencies, crises as well as in normal situations. We need to develop our personality excessively to survive and climb up the ladder of success. A person with developed personality executes his task more effectively than others. Personality development depends on how well we are able to balance and control our emotions to use our inner strengths to the optimum for reaching the desired goal.

We interact with others and our interactive mode is communication. While communicating with others we reflect our attitude, values, inclinations, dislikes etc. These are important elements that shape our personality. When you desire to become a person who everybody will admire you must pay attention to these aspects. Any person with an awe inspiring personality will always be liked and respected by others. When you interact with others, work with others and exchange your views and ideas with them your inspiring personality will support you to gel with them amicably. This way you can be at peace and your inner potentials will get an opportunity to flower. Moreover you influence others by your good examples and make them discover their inner strengths and weaknesses. That is why a person with an admirable personality always is a source of inspiration to others.

Think from another angle. While working in a group, each one of the group members behaves in one's own way. Yet we find the work is accomplished successfully. If you then analyze how it has been possible you will discover an underlying cooperation and smooth coordination among the members that has created the wonder. A deeper analysis will unravel the significance of the personality traits that the members possess. It is either **patience** or **resilience** or **calm tolerance to others' occasional outbursts of emotions**. In the group you may find someone who is ever willing to give and does not wait to take back. All of these persons command respect in the group of people they are working with. In other words the personality of each one of them has played the defined role of **maturity, understanding** and **cooperation**. This explains why it is imperative to groom ourselves for personality development. Whether we work in group or single our personality helps us to execute our tasks competently and successfully. The traits of personality that need to be sharpened and developed are our attitude, interests and knowledge levels that sharpen and develop our skills in several ways.

The professionals, the leaders and the entrepreneurs with a stalwart personality have always an edge over their contenders. A grooming of personality provides them with the drive to interact smartly. They communicate judiciously and carry themselves impressively. That is what personality development is all about.

After you become a professional and enter the corporate world you will find the advantage one, with a commendable personality has over others. One creates an impression by one's manners, smartness, interaction, principles and ethics. Others are simply shadowed by him/her. Your emotional intelligence helps you to achieve all these excellently.

Communication plays a vital role in one's life and it has a significant place in developing one's personality. A person who communicates well is able to impart his messages very successfully to his audience. Communication includes all the subtleties involved in one's body language. The latter is an important component of communication. As such the nuances of nonverbal communication need polish and grooming for enhancing communication skill. That in turn helps develop one's personality.

What impact personality has can be illustrated from the following incident I cite in this context.

Mrs. Ray owns a school. She planned to expand it to higher classes. So she needed to get the information related to the procedures involved and went to the office that provides affiliation to schools. Climbing the narrow staircase she finally located the office and addressed the young lady at the reception in the most courteous manner, explaining to her, her purpose. The lady at the counter did not for once wished Mrs. Ray as courtesy demands. She kept staring at the other end and called a peon asking him to show Mrs. Ray the noticeboard where the details were there. Mrs. Ray felt insulted and came back. What is noticeable here is that the lady at the reception by being nonchalant expressed an attitude that was very repulsive. Attitude reflects one's personality. An individual with the kind of personality the receptionist is will seldom be liked by others. It is obvious one who is happy and cheerful is liked by others and we feel like interacting with him. One who is deployed at the reception must be cheerful and wear a friendly look. Here lies the necessity of grooming and developing personality according to the desired and expected norms. Whatever you do in life you need to be wary about your attitude, outlook and communication style. It does not cost one anything to be polite to everybody but it pays back good name and reputation that one longs for. A smile and a courteous gesture do a lot. They are instrumental in establishing a lifelong bonding.

Interestingly what we note here is that not only the professionals belonging to the corporate need to develop their personality, but any one belonging to any walk of life needs to do the same. A teacher who teaches, a doctor who treats patients, a salesperson who sells, an artist who is involved in the performing arts or for that matter a sportsperson who is involved in games and sports will benefit if he/she is an individual with a charming personality.

One who possesses good personality has a high chance of getting noted. The impression that one creates by a captivating personality is definitely advantageous. Among a class of students one or two become very popular. The teachers, the students, the management committee and others know them by name. While appearing for an interview those few students will feel more confident because their personality is built on the confidence they have of themselves. It is because of this that they have an advantage over others. Their smart appearance, their sense of dressing, their style of interaction and their confidence create an impact on their personality. So you see personality plays such a pivotal role that you cannot help paying attention to it. It provides you with the final touch of being a truly accomplished person. Indeed we cannot overlook the significant part that personality plays in this context.

Personality development does not mean only to look better or carrying yourself better. Yes, they are important aspects of personality development. The salient feature however is something more. Someone with a developed personality becomes a better person with a sensible and rational thinking and a broad outlook. He speaks well and gets along with others marvellously. He is remembered and mentioned always. Even being a high achiever he may remain humble and modest. This precisely is what personality can do.

Let us consider the needs for developing one's personality. Everyone who is either a professional or an entrepreneur has the education to imbibe some values and attitudes in life. One's personality reflects those attitudes and values that one upholds in leading one's life. What about the hundreds and millions of ordinary people who do not fall under the category of professionals? They too need to develop their personality. You feel happy to interact with a person who is endowed with a nice personality. A person with a good personality has an influence over others.

Let us take examples to deduce why we need to develop our personality especially so if we are professionals. Suppose you are a doctor and you are excellent in diagnosing a patient. But somehow or other your patients suffer from inhibitions of fear and doubt to frankly discuss their ailment. The reason is you are quite aggressive and harsh while interacting. That makes them scared and hesitant in asking questions related to medicines and cure. But you are very popular and reputed owing to your expertise and skill. That is why so many patients come to you. However your interaction with them makes them feel apprehensive to approach you. In that case don't you feel that had you been more polite and friendly it would have been better for the patients who harp their entire trust on you alone? It may be you see too many patients a day and it takes a toll on your brain and you tend to lose patience. Yet, if you were patient and poised your communication style and your attitude would change the mind of the ailing people and they would feel comfortable and relaxed.

You see as a doctor too your personality matters and it definitely helps in better interaction. A nurse needs to possess the requisite attributes to enhance her personality for the fulfilment of her job. If you are a teacher you need to be patient, friendly, cooperative with your students to be able to effectively handle the students. A salesperson in a shop needs to extend cooperation with the customers while handling business. In other words if we observe minutely we will find everyone in one's job or profession need to be a good personality to execute the job nicely.

Is it that you want to better a social system that you are disgusted with? Is it that you intend to do something for the uplift of your community? Is it that you want to do something for the underprivileged? Perhaps you want to be a leader to organize and execute your plan along with a group. Whatever you decide to do in life you always aspire to do the job fruitfully. Then you must be endowed with the personality that reflects those key features of a person who has strong determination and urge to do wonders. Whatever you do in life your success largely depends on the kind of person you are. That is the personality you possess.

KEY FEATURES OF PERSONALITY

Ask yourself who you are

Self-image is one important aspect of personality. You need to have proper self-image to make yourself an individual with commendable personality. You ask yourself who you are and the answer will provide you with your self-image. Needless to say you have an idea of yourself but on being asked you will find you are not able to own a complete notion of yourself. The notion that you have of yourself may be entirely subjective, that is how *you* perceive yourself. But the self-image that you must have needs to be congruent with other peoples' image they have of you. If there is a wide difference in their view and that of yours then you need to find out, where lay the difference. An example will clarify what I intend to say. You consider that you are always on time. And you cherish this image of yourself as a person who is very punctual. Well that is fine and absolutely correct if your colleagues, your boss, your clients and even your friends and acquaintances consider you so. But suppose you find out from their feedback that they do not consider you so then your perception of yourself is not congruent with that of your acquaintances. Hence you need to change your self-image. Once you realize your strengths and weaknesses you are in a position to change your perception about your self-image. And then you may try to reform your habit or practices for developing those weaknesses. In fact self-image helps us to gain an insight about ourselves. Often it is rather difficult to form our self-image objectively. As a consequence the self-image that we create does not really help us to identify our weakness and strength.

Let us consider another aspect. That can be the strength of a person. For instance one has exceptional flare for creative writing and he does not regard it as his talent that he can work for and develop himself. He may not make any effort to better it. But proper self-image may make one realize the inner quality that one has and what one must endeavour to develop it. One's talent and hard work help one to grow into an accomplished person that adds to one's personality. If someone else points out to him that he has the strength that he can develop in order to achieve success in life then he can get inspiration to flower his inward strength to attain his goal. Thus it is both strength and weakness that we must discover in us that helps us to form a correct self-image.

It is only when we get a more reliable perception from others can we form the right self-image. We can do that by enlisting some of our successes and failures that analyze the parameters that help us to achieve success and the ones that measure our shortfalls. The analysis will be more systematized if we go objectively and attempt an honest postmortem of our lapses and lacuna. It is true that we cannot be faultless. All of us have some fault or the other and that actually is the reason behind our failure in a particular area.

This can better be explained thus. Let us consider the person whom you regard the most. It may be your brother or your mother. It may be a person who is not even related to you. May be he is your boss whom you respect and regard excessively. However when you probe into the concerned person's personality you will definitely find some flaws in it. Apparently you remain blind to all the negatives that the person has because you have so much of respect for the person. But when you go by an absolute objective perception and analysis you will definitely find in the midst of all the qualities that he/she has, there are some flaws. Then you realize that he/she can better his/her personality by improving or overcoming those flaws. That can be overcome with proper grooming and effort. Some shortfall is bound to emerge when you analyze with penetrative insight. That makes it clear that all of us do have some lacuna. Of course the question here is not with regard to having shortfalls or not, but with regard to the degree or proportion that those wants have and what we do to rid ourselves of that to develop our personality.

It is then that we sum up our negative aspects and decide to work on them. And accordingly we may try to alter our views and ideas, habits and practices to develop our personality and attain success in life. There are social forces that influence the development of our personality. They are largely triggered by imitation and emulation. Human beings learn many things by imitation and copying. So when we imitate we often do that rather mechanically without utilizing our thinking ability. It may so happen that when things are in a flux you do not use your own discretion and you follow others. I have set up a store. My strategies for promotion will be in sync with other players in the same area. Here I go by what others are doing. Even if someone is not doing what I feel should be done I deliberately follow and imitate others' strategies. Here my personality gets influenced by social factors and external agents. We grow with certain elements that are individual and internal and there are certain elements that we are recipients of from external sources.

The external or social factors that affect our attitude and perception are mainly those we imbibe from the ones we interact with frequently as a child. Here the role of school as well as parents is pivotal. When we are children we grow up imitating actions and behaviour that we come across. The parents play an important role in this. Children often are influenced by the behavioural pattern that they observe among the adults. The person they encounter almost regularly during their childhood as coach or tutors perhaps, can influence the personality of the child as external source. That is why it is said that as an adult we need to be cautious and wary of our behaviour and interactions that have deep influence on children. Adults too play various roles in their lives. The professions they are in make them play the role of a professional. Profession and family have different roles to play. The same person as a professional and a family man may assume different roles during the two roles he plays. A performing artist like a comedian or a dancer has perhaps entirely different life style on stage than that he or she has at home. The interaction, the exposure to the world on stage, the experience that one goes through as a performing artist may impose on him/her certain elements of personality that may mould and influence his/her personality. Of course, the basic elements that are *individual* sometimes are irreversible or unalterable by *social* forces.

A child who sees its father or mother in the role of a performing artist will grow up in a different ambience than the one whose parents may be a teacher or an employee in a corporation. At home as an adult we are playing the role of parents, husbands or wives and whatever professions we may be in we have similar roles to play as parents or spouses at home. Now as a child grows up in the environment with parents in a particular profession it imbibes many of the personality traits from the parents. The child whose parents are performing artists on stage or a film star will have some impact on its personality from the parents that rear it up. When two children thus coming from two different backgrounds grow up and ultimately work in the same organization there may be difference in personality to be noted among them as adults. Here what is remarkable to note is that with the influence of background there can be difference in personality that may be quite noticeable in the ways they perceive situations in life. The difference that you see between the two is obviously affected by the environmental factors and the parental backgrounds. There are other factors that affect our personality.

This point can be better illustrated from the examples of the celebrities who perform on the silver screen and their children are able to talk and act pretty smartly. They do not suffer from the uneasiness that may accompany them while they are being interviewed in any talk show. The background and the environment largely contribute to the development of personalities of these children.

Economic background plays a significant role in shaping the values that one has in life. The tendencies of using money or lifestyle that we value depend on the personality we have. One who hails from an affluent class is likely to splurge money often and may not value someone else's idea of thrifty ways of living. Rocky spends ample money in buying outfits quite often. Whatever he sees in the trend he buys that. He goes to the saloon that is the most expensive one. He never goes to college commuting in a public transport. He owns his motor cycle to go to college or to any other place. Every eight to ten months he changes his cell phone or wrist watch. This is the way he maintains his life standard and feels proud that he can afford to do all these. His friends all hold him with awe. The values that he has in fact go to add to his personality.

Vicky is his friend. They study in the same level in the same college. Vicky however is contended with the amount he can afford to spend. He knows he has to spend money carefully and he uses the same cell phone that his uncle gave him when he passed the school leaving examination five years back. He uses an auto to go to college. He has a plain living and he does not have any qualms about it. The way he spends his life has not impeded the growth of his mind or affected his personality. His neighbours respect him, his friends harbour high opinion about him for being an unassuming person and his teachers have affection for him because he is hard working and is not like the other boys of his age group.

Here we have two different personalities coming from two different economic backgrounds. The influence on their personalities is social as the two have different socio-economic backgrounds. Their personalities have various reflections that impact on people around them.

Neither of them is unfavourable or unacceptable. In fact both have their charismatic personalities that are coloured by individualistic elements having been germinated in different social backgrounds.

VALUES AND BELIEFS: OUR ACTIONS AND INTERACTIONS REFLECT OUR VALUES

Two perspectives: Social and Individual in Juxtaposition

Anita and Raj are in love with each other and decide to get married. Raj belongs to Orissa and Anita comes from UP. They have different cultural values as is obvious in India in different states. When the parents of each come to know of it they oppose the union as they feel their children are doing something against social norms. These social norms that we talk about actually influence our value system. Social and external forces go a long way to shape our values and perception. We analyze and judge as per our ideas existing in the form of social recognition. The opposition the families raise is based on the value system they adhere to. The parents look at the situation this way because they have been made to see the way they see, by society. Society tells them that such a marriage will lead to incompatibility. And they view in the same way the society wants them to view. In other words the value system that the parents of each have is imbibed from society. It is not an individual belief or value. May be out of several people one or two will support this kind of marriage. Those one or two belong to the group who have no qualms in cherishing different sets of values being guided and prompted by education and rational thinking that such union is absolutely healthy and has every possibility of compatibility. It may be they have been staying in a different country where they encounter different social values and their perception and values have changed.

Often it is difficult for us to remain unaffected and free from the social agents. You become an object being targeted by social forces like beliefs, perception and values that are rife in society. Your values and beliefs are reflection of your personality.

The values that you have are interlinked with your likes and dislikes. Your propensities, inclinations, desires and ambitions are all propelled by your values and beliefs. Your values you imbibe from your family, community or country. All your actions and interactions are prompted by the values that you uphold. The moral lessons that were fostered in you in your childhood shape your values in life. It is essential that you imbibe values that are respected in society. In corporate governance we find corporate social responsibility plays a vital role. Those too are values that are socially accepted and demanded. Hence it is only desirable that a good employee with a good personality is an individual with fine sense of ethics and noble values. Your personality will gain credence if you show responsibility, integrity, honesty and sincerity at your workplace. When you are assigned a responsible post in your organization, you have to fulfill the responsibility that you have been given. Whatever be the situation you have to execute your task with full responsibility. That is how you can develop yourself as a professional, as an employer and as a family member. Responsibility is linked with relationship existing at various levels both in society and in individual realm that you can think of.

In society responsibility comes in the form of our attitudes and deeds. We can go by simple examples. When there is a disaster befalling the nation in the form of natural calamity like flood, earthquake, tsunami or tornado it is our responsibility to help people who are victimized. Here the help may not be mandatory and we are not enforced by law to extend our help. It is our responsibility that governs us to do all that we do. We are also in a way prompted by compassion that makes us see the plight of the victims of the disaster. Here our value system works and society's mechanism operates on us. Society teaches us and instills in us the value of responsibility by making us a part of the society. There is a collective and organizational work done in such plights or disaster occurring in any part of the country. When you are a member of a social group you automatically imbibe the values that help the mechanism in operation.

Again individual values differ. You do what others are doing. But you may not be interested so much in the work. For instance, if you take part in the literacy drive in which you have little interest or you are not at all keen on doing the job and you do it because social circumstances have induced you to think that it should be done. It is like you have been assigned the job and you are doing it. You do not value the work so much as others do. There is a difference in your value system and theirs.

When there is a festival to be celebrated you find there are individuals who take part quite voluntarily and take the initiative to organize the festival. In schools and colleges you have seen many such festivals where some of the students shoulder the responsibility and do all the necessary work according to the demand. They organize the festival and work hard for it to complete the task. It is not an individual belief or value system that works. There is a social factor involved. Those students who are involved in the work do it with a sense of togetherness. They have been influenced by each other. Here values derived from society have been the inspiring factor. These values help them in taking the initiative and accomplish the task. While doing the task they also become responsible and hard working. They grow the sense of coordinating with others properly so that there is no lapse and they learn to cooperate with each other to end the task nicely. All these help them in developing their personality.

SOCIAL AND INDIVIDUAL

Why Two Perspectives?

There are two perspectives and values imbibed by an individual from two- dimensional sources. They are social and individual. Society gives us the values that we grow up with. Values are related to trends and practices we have. Naturally values will differ from community to community. Marriage as an institution is valued by society in a way that mostly all of us accept and value it from the same perspective. Whereas individually seen we may grow up with individual values in respect to the system of dowry or regarding the bride and the societal acceptance related to her.

In India we have seen a gradual change of values related to lifestyle. The erstwhile values attached to simple living and embracing traditional role of leading simple life relinquishing the earthly pleasures and comfort after a certain age is on the wane. This change of value is social yet some subtle elements of individuality are there. Advances in technology have not only introduced a highly comfortable living, it has also changed our value system to a great extent. It seems there is an orchestration of values and rapid urbanization in our society. With the acceleration of growth in science and technology our lifestyle and trend setting examples have been affected. There are notable changes that take place in the personalities of individuals with the changing generations. Children and youth feel disheartened if their freedom is curtailed. Teenagers enjoy lots of freedom and they utilize their freedom by partying, hanging around with friends and holidaying here and there. The values they have got are derived from society. Their values are endorsed by the general trends that they see around. That is why there is a clash of values in two generations. Their parents may not appreciate the values they have. Here individual value system gets affected by the intermingling of social trends in the air. The social entity that one has is because of the values one embraces in order to be a part of the society.

All these taken together conform to the already existing values and trends in a society. An individual is a part of society. As a consequence he accepts these values and gradually these merge into his views, perceptions and outlook. They in turn shape and form an individual's personality.

There is an important aspect that we need to remember. The sudden change of values or individual cases are just incidental. Our perception and values receive a jolt when we have moral aberration. To follow our moral values with an abiding sense of commitment we must have strong personality not to budge an inch from them. Our value system influences our beliefs and vice versa. If I believe firmly in following the traffic rules I will not swerve an inch whatever be the situation. I may be in a hurry, I may be under tremendous pressure I may see someone deliberately breaking the rules yet I will not violate rules while driving. The reason is, I believe in strictly adhering to my principles and my actions are influenced by my values. I follow rules religiously. That is how I uphold my values in life. And this reflects my personality. This is an example of an individual value that one cherishes and whatever the situation wherever one is one adheres to one's values rather sincerely.

Individual perspectives of values refer to those values that are absolutely formed from inherent tendencies and inclinations. Laziness, introversion, extroversion and excessive demands influence our values. If a child is given too much of indulgence and spared from any enforced discipline during his childhood it may grow up to be demanding. Ultimately that will affect his personality. That will be an example of individual circumstances that is responsible for developing such values in a person.

Similarly we can have many such examples of values having social interface. The values pertaining to trends and practices that we see among people are all social in perspective. The influence of people we mix around in society, their customs and practices, nature and inclinations affect us in forming our values.

You are by nature lazy from your childhood. You do not like to get involved in lots of physical activities. And you grow up with that inclination. That will also bear traces on your values. You would not like to take initiative in any work because you have that attitude to refrain from doing something on your own. You as a professional too would not be proactive and try to limit yourself to the task that your job specification demands from you. You would be happy in doing only the work that is needed and the bare minimum that you cannot afford to overlook and neglect lest it may affect your career. But doing anything extra utilizing your effort and intellectual resource is out of the question for you. The values that you attach to your work affect you. Your values have their root from the natural tendencies you have had right from your childhood. It is pretty difficult for you to shed them now though you have passed that transitional phase from immaturity to maturity. And that is reflected in your personality too. Now you decide on what to do? Perhaps change your values so that you can achieve higher goals in life.

There is however a transitional phase from immaturity to maturity that can sometimes change the values of a person and ultimately help in the development of one's personality. Individual efforts can bring in a change in values.

Many of our emotions are directly linked with our values. Examples are numerous. Intense emotions like greed, temptation, jealousy and malice can distort our values and negate the morals that govern our conscience. You have been always honest and you value honesty as a prized quality in a human being. If you see an employee in your office resorting to forgery for personal benefit, you rage at him. This is an emotional reaction that is followed by your values. The reason is the dishonesty in him. That person's greed has propelled him to compromise his morals and he unhesitatingly commits the offence. The person has to go through a series of embarrassing situations because of the offence thus committed. He will be called for a trial where he may plead himself guilty and he has to face the consequences. This outcome may embarrass him and he may grow an inferiority complex that ultimately results in his poor performance. Here what is interesting to observe is that the two employees, yourself and the other one, have different personalities because your values are so different. The difference in values is obvious. You value honesty and feel that a person's honesty should guide his life's activities. Your value system has shaped your personality whereas his value system has made him what he is. That employee of yours values personal success more than that. He can go to any extent to compromise morals and ethics. He does not have any scruples in committing an act of dishonesty to achieve some temporary gain. This is how one upholds values. The difference in personalities arises from the values one has.

Excessive greed and temptation may lead one to commit severe offences. That may not be individual but a group perpetrating such crime. The various scams forgery, robbery that we learn about involve unfathomably huge amount of money, albeit incurring losses to others. Greed and temptation provoke one to compromise one's values. If one is governed by excess greed and cannot resist oneself from the temptations that one sees all around one is likely to get swayed by the provocations that are mere outward force and external agent. And one proves to be a weak personality when one's mind is unable to fight and resist what is merely an outward force.

There can be lots of situations when you may have to face pressures from sources that are external. If you are not able to cope up with that and unable to oppose what is wrong and unethical then you will be vulnerable to such pressures coming from any unexpected quarter. To make my points clear I would say a strong and decisive personality can always resist those forces that are instrumental in diverting one's morals and ethics. If you are strong enough not only are you in a position to resist yourself you can easily mould others to help them desist from committing immoral acts when they are prompted by temptations.

In the case cited above if the errant employee is given proper counsel to mould his views it perhaps would yield a positive result in future. Values can change if a person is made to perceive the quintessence of righteousness and the glory associated with it. That changes the person's personality too. Greed and temptations associated with power, prestige and money generate quite often from social context. Yet it has another perspective. That is individual perspective. In the same situation two individuals behave in two different ways. Both may have the temptations ahead. But one may fall a prey because of the values one attaches to such situations. The other may remain completely detached and unaffected.

Our personality has another component. That involves our *attitude*. A lady runs a school for children. It is a pre-school usually termed a 'play house'. The play house she owns is located at one of the posh areas of a metropolitan city. Children in her school come from such socio-economic background that they comprise a definite segment. One day she had two visitors in her school asking for details regarding the admission. From their appearance it was obvious that they did not belong to the socio-economic background that the other children come from. Clad in shabby clothes and uncouth in appearance they were in stark contrast to the swanky school they walked in. Be that as it may, the lady who is the Principal greeted them and took them to the office where she addressed them the way she would have done with any guardian seeking information for their wards. The two persons unhesitatingly talked to her and she clearly explained to them what they wanted to know. She has a pleasing disposition. Those two persons were inspired by her words and gestures. They were apprised of the details they were looking for. They had feared that they would not be entertained by the Principal because they were poor, illiterate and were in menial jobs. The lady Principal's values guided her in her communication. Her attitude to them made them happy. This is an example of a person with impressive personality who exhibits rational and sensible approach in her thinking. She is a pioneer of a noble cause in society. Keeping in tune with her pursuit she makes use of her positive attitude while interacting with others. This is the mark and indication of a person with a noble personality.

ATTITUDE

It is always nice to follow the right path and right deeds

It is always nice to have positive attitude

A highly educated person earning a descent salary commutes by train to his office. Often he would purposely avoid buying tickets that is his fare for journey. He knows there is no regular checking at the exit point. Once his friend asks what would happen if he is caught while perpetrating such an offence. He assures his friend that he would pay the fine adding in a mocking tone that the penalty charged is less than the amount he saves in a month while travelling like this. Here what is obvious is his careless attitude that is more intense than his dishonesty. Not that he wants to cheat the railways but his careless **attitude** makes him a dishonest person. Such **attitude** reflects his personality and he will be looked down upon for his stance. His education and upbringing have not fostered in him the positive attitudes that would guide him to walk down the right path that society would respect. His attitude is a manifestation of his personality and it makes him unpopular however scholarly a person he may be. The offence he is committing is unpardonable in two respects. He is travelling without paying the fares thus cheating the railway authorities. Besides, he does not view things in a positive way like a noble citizen of a country. This is definitely a rare case.

In society we find there are individuals with all kinds of attitudes. Some are arrogant and proud. It may be that he is an achiever. His interaction with others, leave behind a mark of arrogant attitude. The attitude may have its root in the values that he has. The education he has received from the environment might have instilled in him the attitude that is not at all commendable. It is a reflection of his personality.

Here lies a problem. The problem is he himself does not know that he is arrogant and haughty and that people often dislike him for his attitude. A right self-analysis will enable him to groom himself to change his attitude. There are some who have an attitude of disliking poor and ignorant. May be the cause is pride and vanity or snobbery. Whatever be the cause there are so many attitudes that are rampant that it make us.

There are both **positive attitudes** and **negative attitudes:**

Individual attitudes are shaped entirely by the influences of parental belief and ideas. Rarely do they get influences from other sources like environment or through social contacts. But it is undeniable that conscience and beliefs are essential components of an individual's attitude to perceive and judge situations. How you talk to someone depends on the attitude you have for that person. But the attitude you have, was developed from your young days.

Individual attitude is influenced by one's education as well. Two persons belonging to the same family may have entirely different attitude to life. Suppose a guy is highly intelligent and performs brilliantly will have one kind of attitudes whereas his younger brother who is not at all academically inclined and hates to study will have different attitudes to life in certain respects. Now when the siblings grow up they may not have much resemblance in their attitudes.

So it is with how you look at a situation. Your attitude to various things in life highly indicates the type of personality you have. An individual with great personality always cherishes positive attitude and clear conscience to gauze everything from an ethical point of view. He tries to instill in his companions the correct spirit and right attitudes too.

Environment, circumstances and situations are the pillars that shape our attitude and develop our personality. We have a positive attitude to many things when we firmly believe in that. Our culture, practices, trends and habits govern our attitude. Attitude indicates an individual's personality. Attitude is highly influenced by one's upbringing. The teachings and moral indoctrination shape the attitude we have. Attitudes of an individual may change with the passage of time and with experience. Interestingly human beings get influenced by various external forces that change their attitude to certain things in life.

A boy coming from a peaceful surrounding will not be aggressive in attitude. Success, happiness, peaceful environment help you to have a positive attitude. If one suffers either physically or mentally one is likely to harbour negative attitude. Culture, demography, religion and environment are those things that contribute in shaping one's attitude. Again one is often influenced by parental attitude. If a boy, right from his childhood sees his father very dominating and influential then he may grow up to be rather aggressive. His aggressive attitude will be revealed in his interaction with others. If he is not checked and if he does not try to control his attitude it will bear impact on his personality. He may become a big shot, but seldom will he be liked and appreciated by others. We know people whose outstanding feat is greeted with great éclat and they attain insurmountable fame and glory. But their attitude of arrogance and vanity always has a negative take on.

Consider the social outcasts like women who are involved in flesh trade. Their attitude to people in general will bear ethos of social milieu rather than anything else. The indifference or impertinence or general hatred for any social norms or for that matter any poignant feeling of sorrow and resignation to their lot is more social in colour than their individual attitudes.

The prisoners behind the bars bear the same kind of attitudes like the social outcasts. They too have been subjected to humiliation and frustration. The reason behind their offences may be multidimensional. Yet the attitudes they have can be generalized to certain extent that they disregard every authority. Their abhorrence is rooted at a social level. The reason is they all are looked down upon and that is why they have perhaps extreme antagonistic feeling clouding their vision and judgment. That governs their attitude in general. May be exceptions are there. But in general they have negative attitudes to activities involving life. The reason is their identity crises in society. These people sometimes develop strong and intense hatred for mankind in general. Their realization and self-analysis is nullified at certain levels. They perhaps have less sanity to think of bettering their life while cherishing such negative attitude.

Your humble and positive attitude enhances your personality. If you are humble you have no qualms about praising others. Even at the face of challenge or competition you show your respect to your contender or enemy. Great leaders like Barrack Obama enthralls his countrymen by his positive attitude, courtesy, and politeness that transpired during the presidential campaigns as noted by Dr Shel Leanne.

Shel Leanne in her *Leadership: The Barrack Obama Way* writes: 'For those observing Obama for the first time, Obama also established a strong early impression with the care he exercised when criticizing the policy positions of his opponent during the 2008 presidential campaigns. Before criticizing presidential candidate John McCain, for instance, Obama would usually first affirm and praise McCain's laudable service to the country and underscore that though they disagreed on policies, he believed McCain to be an honorable man. He would often do the same when commenting about his then-political rival Senator Hillary Clinton.'

This is an evidence of polite and gracious attitude that Obama has. Our modesty, our gestures of politeness while talking to others clearly demonstrate the person in us. That is how we develop our personality.

Many features of personality are enhanced when we achieve success in the work we undertake to accomplish. To achieve success we need to work hard and we ought to have strong determination. But in addition we need to have positive attitude. It is our **positive attitude** that gives us the inspiration to work hard.

A boy was working as a waiter in a restaurant. He did not have money enough to continue his studies. He attended school when he was a small kid. The year he was ten, his father withdrew his name from the school and got him a job in the nearby tea stall. He was helpless. But he did not give up hope. His positive attitude to life made him dream of studying further and make himself qualified enough to take up a job of an employee in an organization. He decided to take help of a teacher who would make arrangements for him to attend school and the accessories required. Soon he joined school and fared so well in the class tests that the teacher was all praise for this boy. His father realized the ability of his son and naturally did not bother him with the job in the tea stall. There was lot of hardship involved. Yet he tried and his efforts were all triggered by the positive attitude he cherished. He cleared his tough exams and passed with flying colours. He will definitely achieve his goal of getting a respectable position in an organization.

Negative attitude on the other hand lets you down. You do not get the inspiration that drives you to the goal. When one contemplates of a situation that he may have to hurdle through to reach the objective he wants to, he shirks it and decides not to embark on the project. This he does out of negativity that inhibits his mind. To be more precise negative attitude works as an impediment for anyone to do anything successfully in life. If you have negative attitude towards anything it will never appear to you as something congenial.

For any successful mission in life you should set a positive attitude to life. That will take you to great heights. Positive attitude helps you to dream, remain optimistic and inspires you to work hard with determination and will. Negative attitude brings frustration and makes you a pessimistic person. You will never be inspired to embark on any great project whether individual or social.

To accomplish a noble mission we need to be very positive in attitude. 'I cannot do it' is a remark given by the ones who are driven by negative attitude and they are the ones who generally fail in their mission.

Negative attitude brings lots of inhibitions in your mind. Fear, doubts, hesitations develop a pessimistic mind and it does not help you. Rather it creates blocks in your mind. Once a negative mind is created it acts as an obstruction and hampers your performance.

There is yet another aspect in negative attitude. If you are not confident and sure about something it is better to avoid doing the work. However it depends on the situation you are in. Negative attitude can be encouraged if you are absolutely free from any inhibition. That is not possible in most of the cases.

Negative attitude makes one diffident. The persistent signal of negativity makes you feel doubtful about your own ability. In this context we should remember that all of us have some inner strength that we need to utilize for our growth. It is a variant that an individual needs to discover and try to work out how that can be his/her way of accomplishing the task needed. Thinking and assuming that you are incapable or fearing to take responsibility in life that may involve trials and tribulations you will not get inspiration to do any task that requires mental, moral and physical effort. Quite on the contrary if you are guided by positive attitude you will find it easier to work with confidence. You will acquire mental strength and that will give you an impetus to work with enthusiasm and hope.

ROLE OF GENDER AND SEX

Gender is a determining factor in shaping attitudes we have in life. Sex here implies behavioural attitude towards the opposite sex. Let us find out how gender affects behaviour, attitude and ultimately, personality. Sex here takes into account the perspectives that are definable as male and female and the relative importance that colours the personality of an individual.

Since the birth of civilization we have seen gender playing definite roles in shaping our personality. A man and a woman have certain distinctive characteristics that are tangible and well defined. You can know a boy from a girl not merely by the looks and physical difference but by their attitudes and perceptions too. Even the mannerisms reflect their basic differences that are there. The noted difference in manners indicates some of the social features and individual elements as well. The 'manly' look or behaviour that we talk about a man is his smart appearance and communication skill. These components constitute the attitudinal behaviour of a man who has an impressive personality. He being a man has imbibed the masculine attitude that has been obtained from his father, uncle and other male figures in the family. Emulating and imitating is quite common among human beings. He may pick up some elements by emulating the iconic male figures in the society he moves around. There are other features like socio-economic background that affects the behaviour pattern and attitudes of a person. Every society has its own cultural values that are reflected in the values that a person is influenced by. That is why we find the attitude of a male is typically different from that of a female.

A lady or a woman has generally the effeminate behavioural pattern reflected in her personality. Here too we observe that community and society as an external agent play a critical role in personality development. The social dogmas inject in woman her values pertaining to marriage, interaction and behaviour. And this is applicable to any community or country. In other words there are several areas where a woman has to accept what society expects from her in order to have the right social identification. So we see a marked difference in the behavioural manifestations of a man and a woman. However it is true that the attitude, perceptions and values are also affected by individual elements that are instilled from other sources like parents and community. A lady born and brought up in UK may have difference in values and attitudes from that of her Indian counterpart. Or someone belonging to UAE may find her female counterpart in the USA too bold and aggressive in attitude so far as interaction with people in general is concerned.

Women who work and are in profession are often found to have certain personality traits that may be in want among others who are homemakers. Women having careers are likely to develop broader outlook and quick thinking ability as their career demands and their outlook and attitude to some of the things are definitely different than women who are not working, looking after the household only and are without career.

Education instills in woman different values and ultimately her attitude towards her opposite sex takes shapes. A highly educated woman thinks more rationally and sensibly and considers herself as no less than the males and her spouse. Her attitude towards the opposite sex is based on equality and sameness whatever values might have been instilled in her and the morals indoctrinated in her.

Interestingly when we talk about attitudes and gender we find differences in attitudes among women towards their own sex. In our society dowry system is so rampant that some mothers do not enjoy the motherhood of a girl child. They feel their daughters are botheration since marriage may later on create problem because of dowry.

Even the mothers-in-law have typical attitude towards their daughters-in-law which is quite universal. Again exceptions are there. Not that all mothers-in-law harbour the same attitude. It is a blending of both at times. Sometimes some mothers-in-law uphold views and outlook that seem commendable as they help in creating strong family ties and bonding. They shed those age old views and outlook germinated from the social and environmental milieu. This change of attitude or views is reflected in their personalities.

OUTLOOK

The attitude in turn gives you the **outlook** you have in life. As Robert H. Schuller says in his *Be an Extraordinary Person in an Ordinary World:*

'It's not a matter of the calendar. It's a matter of outlook. The energy you have depends upon your mood, and your moods depend upon the thoughts you entertain.'

In fact what he means is that the outlook we have depends on the energy we have. **Outlook** is the view that governs our mind, thoughts and impressions on several decisive factors. The high achiever who performs outstandingly and creates a benchmark has the outlook that fosters in him the spirit to achieve the wonderful feat that he aims at. His outlook has been directed by his views that nothing is impossible if one tries. In fact our outlook provides us with the energy, thrust and desire to behave and act in the manner we do. We change our outlook when our attitude undergoes a change. Attitude can assume various proportions and accordingly the behavioural pattern of an individual changes that forms his outlook. The personality of an individual depends largely on the **attitude** and **outlook** he has.

With maturity and age, one's outlook changes. Education too plays a role in change of outlook. Outlook is deeply associated with taste and liking. The taste in regard to choice of outfit or decorating one's house synchronizes with the outlook of an individual. I do not wear western outfit because I have an orthodox outlook. I still believe in adorning myself in the traditional sarees that women wear in our country. I do not have a modern outlook in that sense. For I believe that women should not wear trousers and shirts like their western counterparts. That attire, I believe does not make a woman look graceful. That is my outlook and it may not match with many others'.

I believe in sending my children to public schools and my choice depends on the outlook I have. My neighbour's outlook is different. He considers the missionary organizations preferable and this choice of his depends on his outlook and he sends his children to schools run by the missionaries. My outlook is different from my sister's. I seldom party with my friends. But my sister goes out to party almost every other day. It is her idea of enjoyment when I feel staying at home and relaxing by listening to music is a way of enjoyment. Thus we see ***outlook*** varies and that has different shades and colours for different people.

With respect to gender we find outlook plays different roles. A boy and a girl may have different outlook in regard to some of the aspects of life just because they have gender difference. A girl's outlook regarding her dress and appearance is generally different than a boy's. Girls would be more conscious of their appearance and dresses whereas boys will have no such botheration. For them looks hardly matter unless it is absolutely imperative. This wide difference in outlook with respect to clothes or appearance is a matter of gender difference and attraction towards the opposite sex.

Interestingly we observe that outlook also changes with the change of generations. My uncle and father never took interest in maintaining their physical fitness. But my brothers do. The growth of spa, gym and health club may have affected the outlook of the present generation of males. This gradual change of outlook of males belonging to two generations is absolutely external and is affected by social variants.

Similarly the same may be noted among the females. The women of today cherish different outlook in regard to their beauty and health. What the women in the previous generations did, they would not do. That is because they have less time in going through the elaborate process of health and beauty care. Women in the current generation are busy in other activities and they prefer the visit to the beauty parlour where they get all the care they look for. This is again an example of difference in outlook in two generations.

PERCEPTION

You may perceive it in different way and that makes what you are.

There is often so much of difference in an individual's perception with that of others. This holds true even in case of two persons having the same socio-economic background and education. The fact can be properly analyzed by the organizational behaviour noted among people working in the same organization. Perception impacts your behaviour in a remarkable way.

Zorain and Samit are working in the same bank both as Senior Managers. Zorain would visit his boss on special festive occasions to establish cordial relationship with his boss. Quite on the contrary Samit has a different take on this matter. He perceives the situation in the following manner. If he goes to his boss on the festive occasion he thinks his boss may feel disturbed and may regard it as an intrusion on Samit's part. Two employees having two different ways of perceiving situations behave accordingly. This is not a question of right and wrong. It is just a matter of **perception**.

Jones was a social activist in India and was involved in alleviating child labour. He went to a slum situated in Park Circus. He enquired and found out that the children are encouraged to work from their homes. There are schools that provide them education free of cost and provide lunch. Yet the parents would not send their kids to school. A probe into the matter and discussion unravelled the fact that the parents have entirely a different perception. The children are deliberately sent to work by them so that their children can earn and help the parents by their contribution. Here too there is a stark contrast between the two levels of perception. The government or the ones who are concerned about the welfare and future of the children think that child labour should be removed and those tender children should not be allowed to work. Rather they should be extended the privilege of going to schools and enjoy their childhood instead. So we see there is notable difference in perception in the two groups. The parents of those children feel if their children work they will add to the income of the family. And they do not perceive the importance of children's education or rightful living. The social activists and well-wishers would however perceive the situation in an entirely different way. Perception impacts one's personality.

An individual's perception determines his personality. This is closely related to organizational behaviour where perception plays a tremendously significant role. Perceptual differences may lead to conflict of ideas and opinions. One employee may perceive a situational crisis in an organization as a matter to be avoided and think of staying away from it. Whereas someone else in his place may perceive it from a different dimension and gets absorbed in it with a view to lend his helping hand. The former may have the perception that he cannot identify the reasons of the crisis and is not in a position to solve it. The latter may feel that if he tries and comes up with a solution he will earn credit for it. His perception is in polar contrast with that of his colleague's. This leads to the difference in personalities of the two persons.

Perception also influences our judgment. When we assess an individual we are governed by our perception. There are several elements in perception that form our judgment. For instance a teacher perceives originality in works and projects it as an indication of intelligence and diligence in her students. And she gives more credit to the student who shows originality. According to her perception the student is excellent just because he has originality in his work. She does not attach much importance to other parameters to judge.

Interestingly another teacher may perceive precision and focused answers as the best ones and assessing with such perception she will rate the performance of her students.

Your boss may have the feeling that an employee must be proactive always. That is his perception. Consequently he judges his juniors from that perspective. The perception in him may make him blind and may not allow him to perceive other criteria that may be positive and rewarding in some cases.

The prejudices we have regarding any concept, system or idea are influenced by our perception. Even superstition is born of the perception we have. Biased views pertaining to any social customs or prejudicial views in relation to race, gender, caste, creed or community give rise to conflicts in perception. That ultimately shows in our personality.

PATIENCE AND ENDURANCE

You cultivate patience since your childhood. Patience plays a cardinal role in shaping your personality. You may be fortunate enough to lead a smooth life for a greater part of it. Yet sometimes or other you may encounter trouble or any unforeseen situation that may trigger severe pressure on your mind. What will you do then? You may become impatient and fret and fume because situations are not within your control. How will you cope up with such a situation? Patiently observing a crisis and taking decisions of the following action plan is the only sensible approach to life. Yet how often can we do it?

Suppose you are waiting in a queue for paying a bill. You find the person in front of you allowing others to shove in, and your turn becomes delayed. You are in a hurry too like others. How do you cope up with the situation? Do you act impatiently by pejorative remarks to the one who is allowing others to come in or you patiently wait for your turn? Ask these following questions to yourself

- Do I gain anything by peeving and showing my annoyance?
- Do I lose by being patient?

If you think rationally you will definitely find that you do not lose anything by being patient. Impatience incurs wrath that is detrimental to health. One should consciously avoid it. It pays you in the long run if you remain patient and cultivate patience while interacting with others whatever the situation is. Many conflicts and splits between two persons occur owing to lack of patience and endurance. This holds true both in your work life as well as personal life. Imagine if our mothers were not patient with us for all the tantrums that we threw, how would the world be like?

Ayan is a guy who is posted at Mumbai. He is 25. Staying away from home makes him feel homesick. He does not tell anybody that he misses home. He is brilliant in his profession. He is a perfectionist and wants to run the administrative work meticulously leaving no leaf unturned. This gives him recognition in his workplace and he feels good. However he is short-tempered. He often cannot contain himself and reveals his disgruntled feelings openly. That is why even those who are very close to him point out to him his negative trait. They say he is impatient. One evening he went out to cybercafé to surf the net. There for a trivial reason he had a tiff with one of the members. He did not have the patience to wait for the man to give him his turn. Soon it grew into a scuffle and he was roughed up black and blue by a gang. He broke his nose and had to be hospitalized. What do we learn from this? For a simple reason if one cannot keep up patience one creates unnecessary hassles and that may lead to some serious outcome. We need control and reticence of emotions. Leaders while leading a team needs that. To train our mind and control our emotions we need inspiring source. That enables a leader to steer his team successfully in the midst of all odds. That can be achieved with the cultivation of **endurance** and **patience**.

Endurance helps you to forgive anyone who wrongs you. It is almost a tendency to spite back and retaliate if anyone offends us. How often can we endure if any one back bites us, or harms us by deliberately politicking and spreading rumours against us? The answer is may be not for once. But if we try we may develop our personality by making ourselves more tolerant and patient. Those who have religious tolerance are respected by all religious factions. If you are an achiever you may have to face lots of criticism. And you must learn to accept them with an abiding sense of endurance. Any discomfort whether physical or mental must be endured. If you are able to do that then it will be an achievement and you will be at peace. Everyone will respect you too for your personality.

If you possess the power of endurance then you will not suffer. Most often we suffer because we do not have endurance and whenever anything happens to disturb us we get flustered and irritated because we cannot endure it. As citizens of a country we have our expectations from the government. Sometimes events take place in such a manner that we are likely to lose our patience and power of endurance. At that time the citizens protest in the form of non-cooperation or insurgence perhaps. The reaction is generated from severe discontent and unbearable feeling that they cannot keep in check any more. However this is likely to yield a positive result as history tells us. This is an exception that cannot be ruled out. Yet when considered from a different angle I feel the reward for endurance and patience is much more precious and makes a person a happy and contented.

DRESS AND APPEARANCE

We all **dress** up according to the requirement and situations we are in. Age, gender, climate, culture and situation are the determining factors of how we adorn ourselves. From childhood we are inducted to the dress code that helps us to dress according to the requirement. Yet there are so much of differences to be noticed in the sense of dressing among people. In the same venue for the same occasion different people will dress in their own unique ways. And their appearance will also vary accordingly. Appearance reflects an individual's personality. Not that one has to have handsome looks and god gifted beauty. With a proper sense of dressing, cheerful and smart appearance one can create an impression and command respect and admiration. If you possess a dignified appearance then your personality becomes commanding. You look neat and spruce by dressing cleanly and gracefully. You do your mane properly that suits your look. We need to remember that the occasion suggests the dress we need to wear. In a formal gathering we present ourselves in formal attire. Again in an informal gathering we use casual wear that provides us with comfort. Yet in both these occasions we need to remember that our outfit and our appearance talk about our personality. If you are a leader or a teacher or a person involved in social work then you consider the fact that everybody looks up to you as an ideal. Your appearance counts and it endorses your personality. Irrespective of gender an individual's personality is deeply associated with the appearance one has. The way you carry yourself on various occasions, the way you dress and maintain your personal appearance by a smiling and cheerful disposition and how carefully you observe the nuances of appearing smart and confident indicate your personality. To possess an impressive personality you must have these.

MANNERISMS AND BEHAVIOURAL PATTERNS

Our manners and conduct reveal our inner selves and help develop our personality. Since childhood we learn and adopt our mannerisms. We learn manners from the society we move in. Our culture too inculcates in us the basics of conduct and manners that we imbibe and practise in life. Whatever we pick up as a child stays with us even when we grow up and their presence is felt when we become an adult. Educational institutes too influence our mannerisms. Be that as it may manners and conduct are influenced by our family and then our friends and companions. Education too breeds in us good manners and discipline. A well mannered person is respected anywhere he goes. Manners guide our behaviour and communication.

A well mannered boss never forgets to show his courtesy while addressing his juniors. The way we talk, the way we receive our guests, the way we greet someone over the telephone are some among many interactive modes that are indicators of our manners. Our choice of words while we talk, reveals whether we are good mannered or not. Our body language too reflects our manners. Our posture, our gait, our style of eating and our behaviour at the table while eating demonstrate the mannerism that we have. In fact while dealing with cross-culture ambience and organizational behaviour you need to learn about the cultural trends followed across the world so that you can adopt the expected manners and behavioural norms. That will indicate your personality too.

When you have a discussion with someone you need to be polite and courteous. Your gestures and manners will indicate the kind of a person you are. The way one talks and the way one exchanges greetings reveal the person's inner traits and manners. Even while conversing over the phone we ought to follow the expected courtesies.

COMMUNICATION

The way we communicate suggests the person in us. Some of us can communicate very impressively. Whatever be the language you use, communication bears the ethos of your personality. Your intonation, language, volume and pitch matter while you speak. Whether you are talking to one person or whether you are addressing a group, your communication style reveals your confidence, courage and charisma.

Communication ought to be impressive in order to make yourself an impressive personality. Communication includes conversation, talk or discussion. It can be both formal and informal. When you are having a formal communication it is obvious that you will be prepared beforehand. But even then you need to follow the decorum involved. It is not merely that you talk substantial elements but you also convey it in a polite way. And the other components like non-verbal communication need to be focused too along with verbal communication.

At the core communication involves conversation. When we talk with anyone we create an impression. All of us have definite styles of talking. Here by style I refer to the style of language. The way we express ourselves matters a lot. Moreover good gestures convey good feelings. Sometimes, while conversing when we are irritated for some personal reason we exhibit the feelings, may be not verbally but by our facial expressions. That has a negative impact on others. No one likes to be addressed in a disgraceful manner. Imagine you are talking to a friend of yours who answers with a frown in his face. How would you feel? Surely you would not like it. Nor will anyone. That is why it is extremely important for all of us to be mindful while we converse.

Body language being a part of the communication process we have to pay attention to that also. The gestures and expressions that are conveyed through language are important as that ultimately affects our communication.

ATTRIBUTES AND TRAITS THAT SHAPE OUR PERSONALITY

Consider these attributes: the ones we have discussed that are the components of our personality. All of us have some inherent qualities that need to be developed. We have in us some of those attributes as inherent traits. What we need is to polish and enhance their texture so that they help in developing our personality. We have discussed at length the attributes that we are endowed with but how we can better our inherent qualities and make our personality charming and impressive is our concern.

We can make a self-analysis and try to project ourselves in the shoes of others. Now we discover the areas we need to develop and change. The task is not impossible. If we remember and make an effort consciously we will accomplish the task and reach our goal. Habits and inclinations can be altered according to the requirement. The benefits that we reap by whetting our key features of personality are immense. It can only be summed up by Arindam Chaudhuri's observation in his book: *Discover the Diamond in You*

'A charismatic and pleasing personality is one major aspect of success.'

If you dream of leading a successful life and make a mark in your career then you remember the importance of attitude, values, communication, appearance, smartness and interactive styles that will have a direct impact on your personality. If you enhance your soft skills if you boost up your emotional intelligence and try to develop your personality you will surely succeed in building up an impressive and awe inspiring personality.

NEED FOR HIGH EMOTIONAL QUOTIENT

'Emotional Intelligence helps a person improve his skills and unlock his true potential. Those are the qualities that help a person not only survive, but also thrive in the fast moving business environment. Through EQ, one understands more clearly what motivates us. We are able to more accurately identify and understand emotions and what drives them, which leads to interactive experiences. The ability to understand and control emotions is a valuable foundation to relationships.' viren.naidu@timesgroup.com (Vol. 1 No.29: March 23, 2011The Times of India)

The observation quoted above is by Shiv Khera, founder of Qualified Learning Systems Inc. USA. It provides us with an insight into the functionality of emotion and its manifestations.

Emotions govern our behavioural pattern. High Emotional Quotient gives us emotional stability. Emotional stability helps us to maintain our cool even when we are stressed out. In fact in any crisis emotional stability helps us in overcoming the critical situation. Competition, peer pressure, achieving target are some of the menacing factors that lead to stress.

Even at home we may have differences with our kith and kin with respect to some views and ideas. That may make us feel disturbed. When we receive a sudden and unexpected blow from any corner we may get emotionally charged in an uncontrollable way.

If anybody tells you something that you do not expect you feel a jolt and may be you cannot pass it off easily. That makes you worried or angry or disappointed. These intense emotions assume a magnified proportion and your behaviour is the aftermath. You will be much better off if you can shirk it and remain untouched. That will really elevate your personality and others will endeavour to follow in your footsteps.

2

An Overview of Personality Development

Personality development is essential in guiding one to reach one's goal. It involves emotional control and balance. Personality development entails coordination, cooperation, understanding and right communication. To possess charismatic personality one needs high emotional intelligence. Do you remember any one of your school guys who was very popular among both the juniors and seniors? Can you say why she/he was so popular? When you analyze you find that she/he must have had certain characteristics that made him/her different from others. S/He must have had those fine traits of a distinguished personality. The trait that you still remember about him/her is a person minus outbursts of anger, minus excessive display of emotions of bitterness or disgust or a person with genuine considerations for others etc. In fact those are some of the key features of personality. And because he/she possessed those qualities he/she was so well known and liked by others. In other words he was a well known personality. For developing our personality we need well nourished thoughts that would lead us from immaturity to maturity from the state of naivety to a state of knowledgeable and alert individual.

THE IMPORTANCE OF WELL NOURISHED THOUGHTS IN SOCIAL CONTEXT

Much depends on how you behave and interact with others. In a formal situation all of us wear a garb of civilized and descent being. Yet sometimes we fail to keep up to the expected or desired behavioural pattern or norms. What is the reason? The reason is our thoughts, perceptions and views are not well nourished. We do not have a wide horizon of thoughts that make us perceive things from various dimensions. Our interactions and behaviour do not get the final touches that well nourished thoughts provide us. Consequently our emotional intelligence is not enhanced. Emotional intelligence gives us a space to improve our interactive style and carry ourselves according to the need of the social milieu. We are able to maintain peace and harmony with all others only if we have emotional intelligence that come from our well nourished thoughts. Let us scan and find out what role does well nourished thought have in developing our emotional intelligence and subsequently our personality development.

Examples make an explanation clear. If you are perturbed or annoyed at a situation in the organization you work then your normal behavioural pattern manifests your anger or disturbances that you feel. That is the natural and normal reaction generally people have in times of emotional crisis. The emotions of anger, joyous excitement, terrible fear or agony are often shaped by the environmental factors. All through we need to remember that education and well nourished thoughts help influence the attitude we have towards various things and situations.

A lady happens to stay alone in a metropolitan city. Her husband, a banker is located in another city. The house she stays is swanky. People would often ask her if she feels lonely or scared to stay all alone in her big house located in one of the posh areas of the town. Her house being too big for one person to stay people would come up with lots of suggestions as to how she can utilize the house that seems to be lying idle without being properly used. She listens to all these suggestions. 'Oh! Don't you feel afraid to stay alone in such a big house?' people would ask her. She answers: 'What will I do? I have no option. I am looking forward to my husband's transfer to this city.' She is in a predicament, undoubtedly. Yet she lives through her critical situations in a peaceful manner. This she is able to do because her thoughts that are nourished by reading good books have given her impetus to accept life as it comes without getting affected emotionally.

Your teacher in a particular class has pointed out your misconduct when you purposely responded to someone else's name. You stand up and go on arguing with your teacher and later on avoid attending the class. This is an example of your emotional reaction that is excessive in proportion. You feel it more because it is in the presence of the students you have been chided. You find it too humiliating and insulting. However before doing that you never considered the consequence your behaviour could have had. Now after being reminded of your conduct you become aggressive and do not hesitate to show your temper on someone who is your elder and much above you. Who is the loser can you tell?

It is you. It is you and not your teacher. Here what precisely happens is that you feel helpless and cannot control your emotions that force you to behave in the way that spurts a worse situation. And then it becomes excessively difficult for you to control. And that reaps the consequence. That is why-we need to have a cool personality to be able to confront any untoward situation in life. Let us consider another example.

I wrote my exam paper well but I have scored very low in the paper. I was supposed to have done excellently. I am worked up seeing the marks displayed in the transcript. I go on abusing the authority for being unjust, I blame the university and I criticize bitterly the examination system. I do not eat, I cannot sleep and try to convince everybody close to me that the evaluation system here is unfair and unjust. Do I get my marks altered by dong all these?

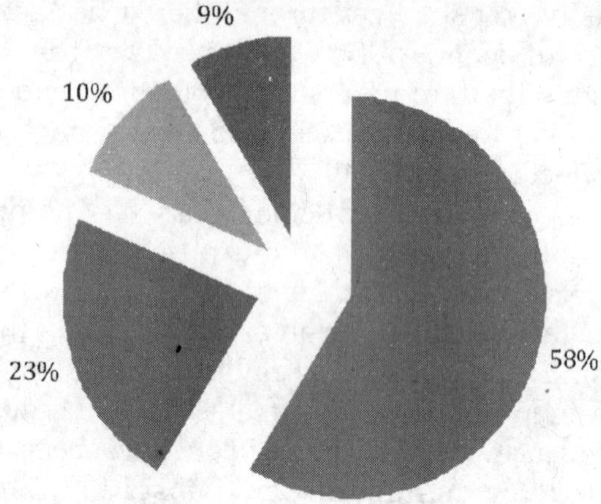

What do I do? Do I blame some outward forces like ill luck or unjust evaluation that has caused this mishap?

Or do I accept my fate and think prudently of my future course of action?

The answer will vary. It will vary according to the thoughts one has. Well nourished thoughts help us in perceiving situations from various angles. And we arrive at a sensible conclusion that benefits us in the long run. Another important aspect related to this is that as we mature from our previous stages of immaturity as we gradually learn from experiences and observations.

While focusing on this aspect I felt how appreciation of culture, art, literature and spiritual upheaval can help in ennobling the vision of an individual in commanding or executing a defined role in life with a finely balanced mind and thought processes. Our emotional quotient will receive a boost upwards if we devote ourselves to art and literature. With a wider mental horizon we are able to think deeper and form a wider perspective. That in fact helps one to call for right decision at any critical moment. It maintains tranquillity in the midst of volatility that gains momentum in the journey of life. Stalwart personality requires extending rapport and full support with anyone he works or interacts with. How can you achieve that? You need to possess stable mind with balanced proportion of emotional involvement.

Success and achievement require proper coordination among team members to enable steer the organization through difficult times. You need high emotional quotient in order to do that successfully. If you are a leader you must remember that creating a cheerful ambience in the workplace is imperative. Success demands upholding high morals and ethics. Success more often than not involves challenges. Each one of these needs to be coupled with emotional balance. When you are embarking on a great project your guiding spirit should be rational and intelligent thinking and not emotional thinking.

Let us look at the pie chart below and consider the position of emotion in the thinking approach of a person.

The chart indicates the smallest fraction (9%) that shows the governing power of emotion that should be in the mind of a person with high emotional quotient when he is involved in thinking and interacting.

Perceived from different dimensions we find striking personality demands emotional stability and control of both mind and behaviour. Since the birth of civilization we have seen great persons from all over the world, display some unique qualities that mark them as different from others. Their intellect, brilliance, knowledge, expertise, communication skill and strong determination have always been coupled with emotional intelligence. In one way successful persons and great achievers share one common trait. They possess high emotional quotient. This they achieve through well nourished thoughts. It is basically their ways of interactions with people, circumstances and various changes they face that make them persons with striking personality.

HOW CAN YOU ACHIEVE THAT

How can we achieve emotional intelligence that is so crucial for developing our personality? Let us consider some great professionals, achievers, celebrities and statesmen who are known for their great personalities and let us see what special qualities they owned that helped them in becoming such great persons and achievers. In fact all achievers have some iconic features of personalities. We can begin with the freedom-fighters those who were inspired with the high ideals of making our country free from the shackles of British rulers. Mahatma Gandhi was an icon. His greatness that makes his personality a distinguished one is that he was assertive in his stance and that made him an achiever. He could think and perceive situation from multidimensional levels. A mind that can withstand stress and remain cool even at crises can think well and accomplish herculean tasks in the midst of all odds.

The first thing that we note is that he was a disciplined person who followed a disciplined life throughout. **Discipline** enables us to do our work steadily and with tenacity. In fact discipline helps one to motivate others to work and lead a life of discipline. Leaders with high emotional intelligence are never erratic in temper and they discipline and train their mind with proper insight to handle and motivate their team. Leaders with high emotional quotient know how to accept changes. They are able to perceive situations more objectively. People with high emotional intelligence and discipline easily shed the tendency to look at everything from their point of view. Political leaders of all times embraced the changes that loomed large. They identified the needs of people and prepare them of the impending changes. Their high emotional intelligence makes them overcome all odds that crop up.

Erudition is one aspect that enhances and sharpens man's intellect and thoughts. A well read person can always speculate over any issue with keen insight and deeper knowledge. Literature helps one to delve down into a panorama of events and anecdotes that transcend the barriers of time. Think of those legendary writers who have created masterpieces that evoke eternal questions related to human life. An erudite person possesses an analytical brain. He/she can analyze an intricate situation in a better way with prudence and jurisdiction.

In a period of transition when an organization goes through a critical phase the able leadership finds its foothold in emotional intelligence. An able person with determined personality does not budge an inch from his strategic viewpoints and retains his calm though he faces opposition from different angles. He can endeavour and bring his mind gradually under control so that he is able to make infallible decisions. An emotionally swayed person on the other hand is hardly able to remain cool defying the odd and adverse situations emerging from various quarters. And obviously such a person cannot be a successful decision maker. Nor will he be an individual with impressive personality.

Here what is called for is strong decision making ability. You achieve this by the application of your **presence of mind**. What one needs most in making an appropriate decision at the moment of change or transition, is farsightedness to foresee and speculate correctly. In case of a decision at the spur of a moment you need presence of mind.

When you are an interviewee you need presence of mind if you are asked questions out of the box. Presence of mind depends on the application of intelligent thinking rather rapidly at any given moment. It is imperative for one to be thoroughly aware of things that take place all around. Information and knowledge pertaining to diverse aspects of life can make one aware and alert.

What does emotion do? It makes us too sensitive at times. We react at paltry and minor things. We show our reactions by our behavioral changes. One whose emotional intelligence is high can overcome any humiliation, obstruction or dejection without a stir. The target objective is the main concern. As a leader we have to attain our mission we have in mind.

What a strong and impressive personality Swami Vivekananda had is evident from the tremendous impact he had had in the Parliament of World's Religions. Many of you know the following story related to Swami Vivekananda's life. He was endowed with a humble nature and noble personality. Swamiji was about to go to attend the Parliament of the World's Religions held at Chicago in 1893. He was not invited. But many of his disciples in India wanted him to go to the parliament representing India and Hinduism. He was indecisive to begin with. Later on he felt inspired and decided to go. When he reached America there was no place for him to stay. What ensued was a tale of struggle. His interactions with the professor from Harvard University who subsequently made all the arrangements for him to attend the Parliament of World's Religions show how his strong determination and vast **knowledge** helped him to create an impression on the mind of the professor. It was his strength of communication that was instrumental in the applauses that were heaped on him. Not for a moment did he lose his calm. He remained poised and dedicated to stay focused to his goal. And while addressing the members in the Parliament of World's Religions in Chicago he communicated to everyone maintaining the grace and proper etiquette. That had an impact that was unfathomable and the overwhelming response from the people assembled there was astounding.

All these leaders were equipped with knowledge and were illuminated with the wide perception and outlook. This you too can achieve by reading good books, journals and articles. Reading widens your perception. It illumines your thought processes and you learn to see and discover the meaning of life.

Meditation helps you to focus your attention to a single object. Our mind is always occupied and goes on incessantly with its thoughts and contemplations. To put a check on that we ought to practise meditation. Technology has provided us with physical comfort. We have achieved so many things in life. However our mind is still racing like tornado for more and more. We need to stop, pause and rest. That meditation can bestow on us. Meditation increases our emotional quotient. We can feel the vibes of soul that connect us with the huge world around where we are just a molecule.

Emotional intelligence makes us perceive situations and circumstances objectively and the bigger issues override the trivialities of life. Think of the dedicated leaders who sacrificed their lives for some philanthropic cause. One name that comes to our mind in this context is Mother Teresa. She remained unaffected by the small inconsequential things and with her poise and restraint she directed her focus on the higher and noble visions of life. She could feel the plight and ordeal of thousands and decided to bring rays of light in their world. She was not merely emotionally charged and cried over their miseries. She worked out a plan and accordingly she proceeded with her work to build up a team like a true leader and ultimately built up the Missionaries of Charity successfully. She is an example of a great personality that we are talking of.

We see many women leaders in the field of politics in the current time. I can cite an example of our late Prime Ministers, Mrs. Indira Gandhi who was known for her graceful personality. In the context we may recall how in moments of extreme personal emotional crisis a successful leader behaves. She experienced the most shocking and tragic demise of her son while she was in the honoured post. Is there any mother who can endure the bitter agony, the excruciating grief of losing her child? Mrs. Gandhi faced that tragic fate. Yet her emotional restraint was evident as she steered her vessel without being overridden by emotion. She could not shirk her duty.

Many of us confront great crises in our life's journey and some of us practise the restraint that helps us to confront a situation without the emotional outbursts. However much grief stricken we are we have to be emotionally calm while executing our decisional role. This is an example of emotional intelligence.

Personality development means this. You change according to the situation that is. You change and accept change that comes.

One of the ways to achieve that is to stabilize your emotions and devote time in thinking from a sensible angle whatever the situation. That can be attained by devouring and appreciating art and literature. It provides you with lots of similar circumstances that might have taken place in that world of fiction yet they are relevant to the situation you may be encountering.

Great personality creates an impact on thousands and millions. With stable mind and emotion you become an idol for so many. They try to imbue your qualities and regard and respect you for your impressive personality. The extreme worries and anxieties that we suffer from are given birth to by excessive emotional involvement. Every human being has emotions. But when emotions overpower a person then it gives rise to imbalance both of mind and body.

Globalization has expanded trade, helped develop the third world and enabled exponential growth in economy as well. National boundaries have been transcended and you see lots of changes that catapult growth in various dimensions. At the same time it has given rise to stress, tension, competitive rivalry, failure, and disappointment. All these cloud the mind of each one of us who marshal a team either as professionals or as entrepreneurs or may be as political personality.

LET US READ FOR OUR PLEASURE

What role does reading play in developing our personality? Before discussing that let us take into consideration some of the fine traits of renowned personalities. We must take our cue from the successful entrepreneurs, orators and leaders. Successful personalities go through the vicissitudes of life. They may suffer from road blocks and culture shock. Dhirubhai Ambani is known for his pioneering work in the world of industries and enterprises. His tale of success reveals the man who possessed emotional intelligence to accept the culture difference he faced while he was working in a different set- up. His varied experience instilled in him the spirit to unlearn and learn the subtle intricacies of human relationship. Besides it helped him later as an entrepreneur. We have scores of names who have achieved success by the dint of hard work and expertise in their domain. And they are remembered more for their magnetic charm and personality.

Liberalization has paved way to frequent cross cultural interaction. Often cross cultural interaction leads to serious problems. You may be vulnerable to emotional stress. You may face too many contenders. There may be variation in cultural values that may breed adjustment problem. Quite often mental stress and tension triggering from inability to cope up with situations cause physical problem. To escape from these you especially need to have poise and restraint. You need to grow acceptance. It is emotional quotient more than intelligent quotient that is required to be a successful person and to sustain oneself in the fast competitive world. If you do that it helps you to develop your personality in the most impressive way.

There are so many unexpected and sudden changes to be found in the environment. Consider those factors that are responsible for catastrophes like tsunami, global warming or the depletion of ozone layer that affect our health and our environment. These result in physical and mental damage to many. In the midst of such natural upheaval when one faces unfavourable circumstances one is likely to suffer and feel miserable. How can the mind be firm enough to withstand all the ups and downs in life? Technology cannot solve all our problems. Quite on the contrary some of the hazards are germinated by technology only. We are entrapped by the fast progressing technology that we cannot do without. The reality has to be faced by us. And in times of dire needs it is our inherent attributes like rational and sensible approach to various circumstances that enable us to confront all kinds of adversity with resignation.

There are man-made disasters too like terrorists' attack, scam, fraud or racial discrimination affecting morals and values of human beings. We are in the midst of all these. Can any leader free a nation from all these? The answer is an emphatic no. What can truly free us from the shackles of nervous breakdown is art and literature. When you are fatigued and stressed out what you need is absolute peace of mind and tranquil ambience to destress yourself. It is then that you resort to a book or a film or music to soothe your mind and body.

To come out from any critical situation in one's professional life or enterprise, one needs tremendous control of emotions. Intelligence and knowledge do not liberate you from all the environmental limitations and hazards that engulf you from time to time. But if as a person you possess the strength of mind and personality then you will encounter all ups and downs without being plagued by them. In fact you will handle situations more efficiently and successfully.

You remember the recession in 2008. The economic slowdown took a toll that was formidable. In financial sectors there were incidents of havoc leading to heavy losses and woes. Firms outsourcing their operations in other countries decided to lay-off a chunk of their employees because business was affected. Doubts and fear of lay-off became rife and professionals were in constant worry. In such situations entrepreneurs whose business was badly affected needed moral strength to cope up with the odd and adverse situations. So were the professionals. News of death and disaster was there in the air. In times of such crisis few could remain unaffected. Great personality means braving any extreme odd and unfavourable situations with stable mind.

Despite all our advantages we reap from the benefits of information technology we need to consider several other areas where we are handicapped by it. And we realize that we must put a check. We have to perceive and understand in a deeper way. Our values need to be strong and proper. Our sense of judgment and discretion needs polish to lend us an intelligent thinking. All these are prized values to develop our personality. They can be geared according to the morals we imbibe from our education and surrounding. Our outlook and values are nurtured by the essence of the indoctrination we have had. A personality who is known and is worshipped needs to adhere to morals and ethics. And that is what developed personality is.

Think.

Technology supports our comfort and easy life. All over the world, especially in developing countries like India growing economy has given a steady rise in the living style of the people. The professionals, entrepreneurs, the leaders and the artists play a pivotal role in boosting the tremendous progress made by the nation. The industrialists of the country have taken the country to a great height by their endeavour and efforts. This is all because of awareness and opportunities that have stemmed from the rapid growth of technology. In the field of education there has been a rapid growth in India. All India Council of Education has initiated the pioneers in education sectors in developing educational institutes in science and technology. They are leaders in leading the country with a vision of achieving phenomenal success in higher education. India produces great number of engineers, technologists, scientists, medicos and professionals in several other fields. This is because these memorable personalities have visions and to reach their long-term goals. These pioneers are inspired by their clear perception and thinking ability.

The peace and stability of mind provide you with something more that you need to have for the completion of your dream project. When you look around you find that you can do something to usher in some change in the society or community you live in. The thinking becomes sharpened when you delve down into literature or appreciate art and culture to glean the imports from them. Art and literature fosters in you the illuminating spirit to think ahead. You can utilize the spirit for your development and enjoyment. That develops your personality.

The idea is provoking that liberal arts has little role to play in the growth of human progress. It is wrong to presume that. Undeniably science and technology assume a pivotal role to lead mankind to an escalating height. Without the rapid pace of science and technology it would have been impossible to reach the height the world has reached today in respect of economy, comfort and exploration of nature surrounding us. Yet when we look at the growth of human civilizations from a holistic point of view we cannot ignore the role of mind and human essence that culture, art and literature help to flower in the seeds of progress.

Now you will be tempted to ask where liberal arts or literature have taken us. To provide a satisfactory answer we need first to consider the contribution of literature in developing the personality of an individual and then the development and growth of human civilization as a whole.

Art and literature influence human minds greatly. An individual's personality is developed with the gradual development of views, attitudes and judgments. The decisive factors that develop the personality of an individual are influenced by literature. Art and culture help develop the fine and aesthetic sense of human mind. Literature is spawned to amuse and entertain. That is why it is easy to be influenced by it. When you read a book you know it is a work of fiction. It may also be a book on information pertaining to a domain. It may be a hilarious comedy that lightens your mood and takes away the pressure that you may be going through. Again if you read a serious theme that revolves round some events like deception or treachery in a relationship it will have a different impact. The interesting part is the author does not pose his or her views. You develop your own judgments and try to identify the vice and virtue weighing them against the values that you have imbibed. Here literature plays a significant role. It directly impacts your sense of judgment and values. Our judgment and our values often get a larger dimension when we read various authors belonging to various times. A work of art like painting or sculpture provides us with sheer joy. We appreciate and admire a painting. Of course it is only when we value the work of art that we can appreciate and our aesthetic sense intensifies. In the office you face the pressure of targeted goals. You remain too much disturbed owing to that. Why don't you try out a good author? It will give you relief and joy.

I recently met a Mumbai based lawyer who is young and dynamic. He is a criminal lawyer. He narrated some of the interesting cases that were horrific and deplorable. I wondered when he said, 'Sometimes charges for harrowing cases of murder keeps me working till 2 o'clock at night and again I start working from 5 the following morning. This is quite a frequent schedule with me.' Such work schedule tires him and he feels worn out. He finds respite from it by writing. By now he has authored two books. He also is an avid reader of books. In fact literature has kept him motivated spiritually. That is his way of keeping himself calm and stable. One needs to be stable emotionally to reach one's goals. That tells on your personality.

People you meet are of various types. You interact with them and sometimes you may be affected by their words. How you retain your calm is a big question. All you have to do is to try some of the ways to stay calm and put a rein on your emotions. You can listen to good music. You listen to any song or tune that soothes your heart. You may take a book to read or you may pour yourself into a poem. That will give you pleasure and will relax your mind. You will gradually develop self restraint that will help you achieve emotional balance.

In fact I feel anyone can try to achieve that. All of us who lead a life of stress and strain can easily acquire stable and balanced personality by cultivating the ways to achieve that. You read, sing or play musical instruments or if you have the inclination and of course if you have the taste for drawing and painting. You can enjoy the performing arts to release your mind of the pressure that may generate for some reason or the other. That helps in the following ways.

You get a penetrative insight into human nature and mind. After all it is the interaction with human beings in society that breeds pain or pleasure. All human relationship revolves round various emotional manifestations. A person with developed personality is an inspiring agent. At the same time a leader is subjected to lots of criticism. The reason is obvious. The ones she or he is leading harbour strong faith and hope from the leader. If there is an iota less the followers or the coworkers at once shower their ire and discontent.

Let me bring those pictures that will immediately remind you of various similar incidents you have experienced in life perhaps. You have done a project that was a group work. You did the main work since you were the leader. However when the final work was to be compiled you took a day extra as a result of which the work was submitted late. Your group mates point their fingers on you stating that because of you they got their work late. They forgot the hard labour that you gave throughout. They remembered your failure without appreciating your fruitful contribution.

It is natural for you to feel hurt. However if you can control your mind you will find you are not getting disturbed. Rather you gain peace and happiness.

Some of the things that you can do to develop your personality

The HR head of Tata McGraw-Hills Education Pvt. Ltd conducted counselling sessions for the employees of her branch at Noida. The session was conducted for the high potential employees. Over a cup of coffee she went on telling me some of her interesting encounters with the employees who are labelled as high potential employees. Her experience revealed the following:

Some of these high potential employees have no short-term or long-term plans. On being asked what their short-term and long-term plans are they are unable to provide any immediate answer since they do not have any. They are happy here today. For tomorrow they have no plans. They lack a planned and methodical way of career growth. It is obvious these people will have difficulty to face a sudden change of policy in the company since they have no fall back plans for their future. Professionals face critical situations when it is difficult to galvanize them properly.

Who is a person with an impressive personality?

You are. You can be the person if you so desire. You may achieve that by your smartness in looks and thoughts. Great persons are the ones who are specially endowed with abilities and desire to perform a task. They lead and show the path of excellence. Engineers, doctors, lawyers, teachers, artists and composers are all great persons. In their workplace they lead and coordinate with the team they are working with. They are leaders. When we consider the term 'leader' in its comprehensive view we include a myriad of people who have very different areas to work and interact. They are the ones who contribute extensively to the development and growth of civilization. They lead the nation and the world by their contribution to their professional field.

A doctor is a professional who serves mankind by the application of his knowledge of medicine. In times of critical ailment one rushes to a doctor to seek his medical advice. The doctors in the field of research contribute by their fruitful findings that help cure diseases. The surgeon while operating on a patient works with a team of assistants. It is imperative for him to execute his task coolly at the moment. And for that he needs to retain his poise. He is not only working in coordination with his team, he also makes use of his expertise and skill. And all these need to be clubbed with his emotional balance even if the situation goes out of his control.

A journalist is a professional. He writes or blogs for the media. He needs to present facts with the objective of telling people all that happen in the world around. He has to be scrupulous in his presentation of the text he writes. His discretion will be propelled by his rationality and sensibility that come from the right magnitude of emotions.

The musician or music composer too is a great person. His/her outstanding ability and talent help him/her to attain glory and his/her work of art is a source of joy perhaps to millions of people. It is also a source of inspiration to lots of future musicians. And he/she enjoys being a person who is admired and respected by his/her fan followers. He/she earns fame and celebrity status. However his/her personal dealings with people reflect how high his/her personality is.

A teacher is a leader who amasses a storehouse of knowledge to give to her students. His or her knowledge enables the student to be enlightened in the field of study the teacher takes up. The teacher often becomes an ideal who is an inspiring agent for her students. Definitely she needs to be an epitome of patience, forbearance and affection to teach. All these germinate from her high emotional intelligence and her personality.

An engineer works for the organization that helps in developing and maintaining the diverse resources and institutes of the country. A software professional contributes immensely by designing or developing software that leads millions of people to work with efficiency and smoothness. A software professional writes programmes that break new ground and enable further development much efficiently and with rapidity. He must work with dedication and devotion to be a path-breaker in the field of knowledge where he plays the role of a leader. But when it comes to making an impression it is his personality that is called for.

The dancer is a professional who amuses and entertains her audience by her graceful movements of body that reveals her fine sense of creativity. A musician hones his latent per se by perseverance and creative spurts. This makes him establish himself as a reputed professional in the field of music. A painter too devotes his time by creating marvellous work of art for the world to enjoy and appreciate. All of these above professionals are known for their expertise in their special domains. And they are leaders.

They are leaders in a sense that they are leading in their specified domain their juniors and their colleagues who follow them. Yet they need to have something more than the skills and knowledge they possess. It is the personality derived from the ethos of literary art and culture that endows them with the essence of human beings. That helps in developing their personality.

Professionals as leaders use extensive knowledge, skill and expertise in their specified areas to work efficiently. So are the entrepreneurs. The same thing is with the political leaders. Technical knowledge or business acumen give you a platform but your personality helps you to have an edge over others.

As professionals you need to be dynamic, thought provoking and percipient in order to grow and help the steady progress in the field you are working. The technical expertise the professional as leader acquires is on the basis of theoretical knowledge and orientation. The application of the knowledge calls for a host of elements that take birth from the essence of emotional quotient. We have explored how that happens. The knowledge base is one important component of a person. There are other elements that need to be accompanied with the knowledge base that make a person successful in his mission of reaching the wide horizon that he dreams of. A successful person in his profession is inspired by a wider and wider horizon that prompts him to reach one goal after another. However there is something beyond that. It is not always that you crave for the fulfilment of your personal dreams. You may be looking for something more. That is an elevation of mind and spirit that will give you that 'something' which you still have not been able to get. You can get it by exploring the inner self through meditation, reading and listening to soul stirring music that creates a tranquil feeling in you.

Mr. B. Ghosh was the director of IBS, Kolkata a reputed institute offering MBA Program. He was leading his organization. He is a man with brilliant academic performance to his credit. He was dynamic and had vision of steering his organization well. But he had no patience. He could not patiently hear his colleagues talking about something important. He would easily get impatient with them rave at them and rankle for petty reason. This alienated him in the organization and his junior colleagues talked against him behind his back. Within a year many of the faculty members put up their resignations and the attrition rate grew high. The institute suffered badly. Soon he was asked by the headquarters to give a reason for the deplorable state of the organization. Ultimately he was removed from his chair. He became an unpopular team leader because of his lack of personality.

An individual with an impressive personality is without **prejudice** and **bias**. When you run an organization you must have everybody's cooperation. As such you need to observe all the team members thoroughly. That has to be without any prejudice and bias. A successful team leader is not influenced by anybody else while forming his opinion about a member. He should see everything objectively before coming to any decision. Biased views and prejudices lead to distorted opinions that may ultimately culminate in embittered relationship. You have to find out everything objectively. That will make you a likeable person. The mind of a leader should not be subjective while inferring anything on the basis of secondary information. It has to be absolutely clear while perceiving any situation or judging any person. What would you do as a leader to be an admiring personality?

Set aside your emotions and try to solve problems by drawing inferences on the basis of facts.

'All were glad: the plants, the birds, the insects, and the children. But men, grown-up men and women, did not leave off cheating and tormenting themselves and each other. It was not this spring morning they thought sacred and important, not the beauty of God's world, given to benefit all creatures — — — — a beauty which inclines the heart to peace, harmony, and love — — — but only their own devices for getting the upper hand of each other.'

Resurrection by

LEV TOLSTOY

Human nature is full of intricacies as is obvious from the quotation above. They are governed by malice, revenge, hatred and envy. The writer who pens down thoughts of eternal and perennial appeal has been read by millions of people. Lev Tolstoy's observation on human nature reveals an element of profound truth. It makes us perceive life from different angles. A novel that depicts such penetrative insights into human psyche helps its readers to understand life in its subtleties and complexities. Your thoughts become vivacious and exuberant with deep perception of life that you acquire from literature woven in well nourished and astounding facts. A person derives his inspiration from such well nourished thoughts. What Tolstoy has said is the reading enriches our mind and we derive pleasure by reading. In any profession we need to think. Profession is a specified field of work. Quite obviously one, who works has to contemplate, reason and infer for successfully carrying out his work. There is no place for emotions and sentiments. The surgeon who performs a surgery knows the nuances of surgery that he is going to perform. But for that matter he cannot operate on a patient without prior contemplation of a series of factors that are to be organized. Here consistency of thoughts and actions go hand in hand to the successful completion of work. A film maker goes on with the thinking project of his script, cast, crew resources and so many other paraphernalia. When we consider the consistent thinking we imply a good thought process that needs to be well nourished. Thinking is a continuous process involved in a profession. A teacher when teaches has to know her subject matter much before time. She collates facts to supplement her subject matter. And while teaching she has to think of the relevant questions she may be facing.

How do they improve their mind and thinking ability? They have one good resource that is literature. Literature is like a door that leads to the threshold of an enlightened world.

WHAT IS ESSENCE OF LITERARY THOUGHT?

Let us scan the essence of literary thoughts. The first question that strikes us is what is literary thought and what role does it play in the life of a professional and an entrepreneur. Literary thought refers to the ethos that is strongly embedded in a text that comes under the genre of literature. Literary thought is the underlying perception of the creator of a book as seen through his or her perspective. This underlying perception is the perception of life in its varied forms and manifestations. The 'perception' or perceptions that the millions of books in the treasure house of knowledge have, present a plethora of facts involving humanity. A well read person must nourish his views and thoughts with the perception that the liberal arts or literature lends him. So varied and diverse are the thoughts and imaginations of human beings that one who delves down the world of literature comes out with an enriched outlook in life that would influence his outlook and values. A person may not have the opportunity to travel the world extensively but by reading literature he may acquire a multidimensional perception throughout his life. Literature curves the thinking and rational faculty of the reader. A good book is a gateway to great perceptions. All of us possess the ability to perceive situations in our own way. Literature encourages us to perceive situations from various angles. We may be led to view things from an individual's perspective as presented in the book we read. This helps. You as a reader discover that your perception has broadened and your belief and attitude change along with your perception. You may discover that your sense of judgment and discretion have assumed a different proportion. This develops your personality. A successful entrepreneur or a professional in an enterprise is greatly helped when he or she is endowed with a fine sense of discretion and judgment.

An individual's personality reflects his/her attitude, outlook, values and perceptions in life. Whether a person is an entrepreneur, lawyer, doctor, professor, journalist or a film director it makes a lot of difference if he makes him more pronounced by his personality.

Your personality differs from your friend's. Why? Do you know? Each one of you is reared up in different families. Each one of you has imbibed parental values. It happens like this that as a child the first seed of conscience that germinates in you is the effect of parent/child transaction. As a child grows the values remain but they may not be perpetually present.

How can one develop one's personality? The answer is he must be well read. A person who is well read in literature has his perceptions widened to a bigger horizon. Literature is a reflection of life. It is easy for a reader to identify those aspects of individual problems that constitute human life that literature presents in the guise of fiction.

Besides he knows how to speak in an impressive manner. Organizational communication is an important area where the professionals and the entrepreneurs have to possess the required skill. Communication whether formal or informal has a very significant role to play. A well read person improves his linguistic skills by his avid reading. That helps him to talk in every situation appropriately. A well read person can bring in relevant instances while explaining anything. He can quote eminent personalities if required. He can give touches of humour while talking. He uses the fine language so that it does not hurt the sentiment of others. And the most important thing is he can use his expression in an apt manner that conveys exactly what he wants to convey. We all recall the great orators all over the world for their captivating speeches that are their adornment of their personalities.

3

Emotional Manifestations

How do you react in similar situations?

'You perceive yourself to have been insulted by someone and thereafter your whole thinking about that person is colored by this feeling. You perceive (perhaps falsely) that someone is saying something out of self-interest and thereafter you discount everything that person says. You perceive something to be an advertisement and thereafter withhold belief. We are very quick to make these snap judgments and to become locked into the emotions they release.'

—Edward de Bono *Six Thinking Hats* (Chapter 2)

The father of the concept of six thinking hats has in the context of discussing red hat stated the above. It is clear from this observation that human beings are often prompted by emotion rather than logical analysis to arrive at a conclusion. We see many great emotional eruptions taking place owing to our arriving at impulsive and abrupt conclusions on the basis of something that does not have a strong ground.

Do you know we are all bundle of emotions? We cry, we laugh, we seethe in anger, we are overjoyed and we are disappointed at various moments of our life. Any outward force can easily germinate the seeds of emotions. And then follow the revelations of our emotions in a magnified version. This causes us to react emotionally sometimes in an amazingly high proportion.

In this sate when we interact with others the latter bear the brunt of our emotional reactions.

Any emotional manifestations in an extreme form generate discord and disturbance in the mind of the emotionally affected person. The aftermath of the response is most undesirable. It is more so if it involves other persons. Being excessively emotional we show our reactions in such a manner that it becomes quite embarrassing when we recall it later on. We interact with everyone around us and our emotions influence our manners, behaviours and communication style.

Of course it is natural and quite human to be emotional. When we experience some good events affecting our career or our life we feel the happiness that generates emotions of joy. We feel extremely happy when our kids do achieve excellence. Again if anything happens where we suffer great loss or experience misery then we are affected by emotions of sorrow. And there are expressions of these feelings that are reflected in our behaviour that are called emotional response. There is nothing to cause concern as long as we express our emotions in a sensible and in a moderate way that do not affect our behaviour and opinions. The emotions that we manifest through our behaviour and gesture and the way they affect our thoughts and ideas are crucial. Emotions should not guide us entirely in our formation of opinion or inferences. Rationality and sensible approach are essential for our thought process and opinion. When we are swayed by emotions and that cloud our vision and judgment then it becomes a matter of concern because that affects our personality. That is what we call 'excessive emotion'.

You are prompted to ask perhaps 'How does it matter if I get overjoyed after I win a victory and am declared a champion in the contest where I have beaten so many potential singers and I jump and reel around on the stage to exhibit my feeling?' Well there is nothing wrong in this because it does not affect anybody. But the ones who see you behaving in this way will feel you have no control over yourself. You imagine the situation objectively. There are two singers in two groups. Both have topped his own group and have won the title of the champion. Their feelings in this respect are the same. But the emotional manifestations of the two are totally different and they behave in totally different manners. One like you gets overexcited and displays his excessive emotional behaviour in the way you described, whereas the other one remains calm and feels the joy without displaying any extreme behavioural manifestations. The reason for this difference in emotional expressions is their **personality types**. Cultural differences are there. One may remain calm with a subdued expression of emotions of joy whereas the other may exhibit the same with exhilaration of mirth. They have different cultural values and that is why their personality is so different. Obviously the one who is able to control himself will be appreciated by the others. The one who is overenthusiast will appear a little less charming than the other. The one who can retain his calm and can control his emotions will be regarded as a descent person.

You come across people with such diverse emotional responses and reactions that create an aura of emotional display. This can very well be observed in a public performance when performers react in different ways when the result of their performance is declared in a public forum. We can also note the behavioural difference of a person when a situation takes place to make him angry. He may express his anger by outrageous behaviour without being able to control his anger. We see in an accidental mishap one in extreme plight screaming and crying for help without being able to decide what to do and say what has happened. We have numerous examples where we find uncontrollable emotions cause harm and destroy relationship. We all have witnessed various levels of emotional outbursts from one individual or the other. People sometimes are so swayed by emotions that they cannot contain themselves. They lose control of their gestures. At that time they do not realize the harm they cause to themselves as well as to others. What is very important to note here is that the unguarded emotional expressions make you a weak person. On the other hand proper control of emotions enhances the growth of personality.

Let us take an example and see how extreme emotional response can affect a relationship. In a rage of anger you may say lots of things that you might not have said to your neighbour who invariably parks his car in front of your house every night causing you inconveniences when you go out the following morning. Now when you say something your friendship with the person is strained resulting in the embittered relationship between the two neighbours. However, if you explain to him that it causes inconvenience to you that will solve the problem in a better way. He will realize his mistake and will not repeat the action. But if you were to show your annoyance it might have taken a worse turn. Useless feud spoils the relationship that results in unhealthy ambience. Your endurance and gentle behaviour on the other hand will be an eye-opener not only to the neighbour who has been insensible and behaved in such a way. The others too would note your good quality and behaviour. Your personality would be awe inspiring to them. You attain popularity respect and goodwill from your neighbors.

Appreciation of culture in the globalised ambience

Appreciation of culture relates to your empathy and respect for diverse cultures that are becoming so palpable because of globalization and liberalization. People belonging to various parts of the world have their diverse sets of culture and practices. In the present situation any professional has to be in interaction with one belonging to the other side of the Atlantic. Your appreciation of culture of various nations and community across the world will enlighten you and you will find it easy and comfortable to work and interact with people in different situations. As a professional or an entrepreneur, that will help you and it will benefit you in achieving success. That will help to lead a comfortable life.

It may so happen that you are a performing artist going to perform in different places where there are entirely different cultural values prevalent among people. Will it not be useful if you acquaint yourself to the culture of those people in front of whom you are going to perform so that you can make an impact among them in an appreciable manner? That will help you to know and interact better with the personality types of the people with whom you are going to stay and with whom you are to work. That will make you less **emotionally charged** perhaps since your acquaintance with the culture of the people will give you an insight into their tendencies and practices. That is why it is important for us to know the diverse cultural practices and values of people of various parts of the world. That develops your personality too. Your emotional intelligence is increased in the sense you respect and value the cultures of others removing the erstwhile inhibitions you might have had. You enjoy being in any part of the world working and interfacing with people from diverse cultures and values.

A magician like P.C. Sorkar may go to perform at China. People invite him and he accepts the invitation and goes to China to perform. The members who are organizing and managing the show are all people belonging to China. They welcome him and interact with him retaining their style and cultural trends. A celebrity like Pandit Ravi Shankar, the sitar maestro must be able to reciprocate and interact in an amiable way wherever he goes to perform. There may be differences in various things that he encounters in a foreign land. The subtleties and nuances pertaining to cultural values of the people there and those in his country may have a wide gap. However by being friendly and warm among the ones he performs his show, he will be at ease and he will be respected and regarded with admiration. Gestures of warmth and appreciation of others' culture help you to earn respect from others. That is possible only if you never react being governed by excessive emotions seeing anything that you are not accustomed to see in your own community and culture.

Suppose you are an entrepreneur. You have your business operations across the nation. It can be across the world even. Your enterprise will thrive if you encourage your employees and show your appreciation of their culture by your gestures and interactions. Your business will grow if you care for your employees and respect their cultural values. Human resource of an organization is the most precious resource for the growth of an organization. As an owner of a fast growing organization you ought to set an example by your religious tolerance, respect for others' culture and sentiments attached to it. That will develop your personality and it will help you to earn respect from them. They too will be imbued by your attitude and your personality.

When you interact with someone belonging to Japan you read and learn about the cultural trends practised and rampant among them. Your knowledge about the country's cultural history will help you to gain adequate acquaintance with the cultural trends that the Japanese value. When you go Australia or UAE you will find differences in trends and practices among people in those places. It is obvious. If you go and stay in the USA you will note the difference that their culture has. Your adjustment and accommodation will rest on your ability to accept everything with a good heart and warmth. If you feel the difference is an issue and you cannot adapt yourself for the sake of convenience and successful execution of your task then you will find it uncomfortable and you will not like the ambience created by those around you. You are likely to have emotional reactions that may assume formidable proportion at times. So to safeguard your respect and stance you must be familiarized with the prevalent cultural values of the native inhabitants wherever you go or stay. If you change your views according to the need and feel you can accept what they practice and do in their social context then you too will earn their respect. They will regard you as an individual with an impressing and pleasant personality.

People respect you for your personality and regard you as your friend when you extend your fellow-feeling with them. That will help you to successfully interact with people in the country you go for your professional aims. Moreover your personality will be greatly developed with your value addition. Knowledge gives you power and it adds a different dimension to your personality that will be admired as awesome and inspiring. People will respect you for your dynamism, attitude and willingness to change.

Imagine you are a doctor who deals with a large group of patients in a cosmopolitan set-up. Patients come to you from different backgrounds. And they have different cultural values. Hence while interacting and diagnosing you have to behave with them maintaining the uniformity in attitude and views. Your norms of behaviour and interaction are influenced by your generosity and wide visions that you have. All these enable you to create an impression among the patients you deal with.

Your appreciation and empathy for your patient makes you an admirable doctor anywhere you practice and meet patients.

Kolkata is known to be a place where spectators in the sports ground display excessive enthusiasm. That may create a feeling of surprise and astonishment in the minds of the international players coming from abroad. However if those players are acquainted with the prevailing culture here among the sports fanatics they will probably not suffer from any misgiving or skepticism. Quite on the other hand their appreciation will make them endearing to the hearts of thousands of spectators. Making your personality admirable means you need to extend your cooperation and coordination to everybody around you. And when you are able to bring about a change according to the need and demand to make yourself acceptable then you are able to reach your desired object. You own the personality that everybody respects.

Wherever you are, you find the difference in culture, societal values or religious perspective or may be educational background in various places quite noticeable. Knowing the difference is very important. That will ease your problem in interaction. People will like you and you will be remembered for your personality.

Reading literature helps you. It is a mode of entertainment. Fiction in the guise of a story unravels some serious aspects of life. Unlike didactic literature fiction does not need to tell you this is wrong and this is right. The reader is transported to that realm of fantasy from where he can glean the truth that is universal and perennial. And while weaving the world the writers create their human characters with multi levels of emotions constituting the entire canvas of human world. You are transported to that world and you see with clarity those elements that constitute human emotions.

Think of any Indian writer who writes novels. His or her work will be a reflection of the country he/she belongs to. The Nobel Laureate Rabindranath Tagore wrote inspiring novels in Bengali to unfold some of those issues that would evoke and create a stir in the minds of the reader and would point out the plight of the victims who were subjected to social dogmas. Unless and until we read Tagore we cannot be critical or thoughtful about those aspects of life where we identify the problems that affect people at large in society. Lots of emotional response is involved here. A writer creates his own world where permeates the ethos of social issues. The work of the author helps you to know and discover some astonishing facts perhaps related to the society of the community the story revolves round. That provides you with an insight into the foibles of society that affect people. Then you can draw a margin where you perceive the variation existing in society and you are able to compare and criticize. Awareness comes from observation and reading and that makes you a man of thought and keen perception. A well read person is an adept in thinking, talking and judging with prudence and intelligence. That makes the difference in personality.

If you acquire the key features of an impressive personality you can through your knowledge and vision impact your neighbours, country or community the author is talking about. Similarly you get a penetrative insight about the historical or may be social issues from the work of a writer. Social issues pertaining to the time the writer is writing about unfold to the reader as the book progresses. The excellence of literature lies in the fact that it appeals to human beings since the sequence of events is given a deft touch by the author.

Unlike history or social treatise literature creates an ambience of thrill, suspense and curiosity for the reader to know the subsequent events till the end. That is why we talk of literature because anyone can read that.

We have discussed in detail how essence of literary thoughts enhances our vision and help develop our personality. Literature is the mode of entertainment. A literary artist serves both the purposes that we desire. We derive pleasure and we are enlightened by the underlying thoughts of the various issues a literary work may provide. Charles Dickens wrote his novels that depicted social issues in the guise of stories that are fictitious. The ordeal of the orphans placed in the work house or the indirect impact of Industrial Revolution during the early part of the nineteenth century or *his A Tale of Two Cities* portraying the deplorable and miserable plight of the prisoners unearths the historical events associated with French Revolution. History will tell us all these in detail. But how many students who are doing graduation in micro- biology or for that matter doing graduation in information technology will go through the details of history? A few among them may be out of interest read the facts related to some great upheavals, revolutions and wars in history. The social issues or historical events leaving behind far reaching impact are often merged in literature. Only when we read literature out of interest that we discover them. They however are truths that are delineated by the creator of the masterpieces like *Oliver Twist* or *Great Expectations.* Similarly when we read Victor Hugo's *Les Miserables* we perceive the intense and profound truths underlying the storyline that gnaws us from within.

It is not merely social or political or cultural aspects that we discover in a literary work. There may be still more relevant aspects concerning human life that are woven in the scribe. Let us consider some of the legendary works that are classics in literature. Shakespeare's *Romeo and Juliet* for example tells us the story of passionate and intense feeling of love that defies and transcends all barriers of social and familial inhibitions. Remember this problematic issue seen from the perspective of literature is not confined to specific time, societal and political background. They have their perennial existence irrespective of time, country or religion. That is why literature is said to have a wide horizon that evokes in us so many questions. Those questions make us ponder over the numerous issues that we come across even today. We learn from facts that are proved on the basis of experiments or observations. Facts teach us things that are there in the surface. Fiction makes us perceive things that surface from the maze of imagination that the writer creates. We feel and perceive. That perception governs our emotions as well. After reading *Romeo and Juliet* we wonder and think whether the two families, Montague and Capulet, have been instrumental for the tragedy that took place. The tragedy invokes questionable issues related to one's perception and values. At the same time you will find readers may have quite controversial opinions pertaining to some of the important questions thus raised from the tragedy.

Rabindranath Tagore's *Gitanjali* captures the heart of the reader because the poems make the reader see the Almighty as omniscient and omnipotent agent where one can seek salvation and feel the heavenly bliss in life. His dedication and devotion to God is expressed with an ineffable joy. Here you are ushered into the realm of metaphysics woven in rich and elevated thoughts that permeates the mind of the poet.

You only need to appreciate and understand the sublimity that there is in literature, art and culture that will ultimately make you extract the pearl underlying beneath. What effect will it have on your personality?

It goes without saying that a person well read has an enlightened vision. It enhances his mental growth and broadens his outlook.

Besides being a source of intellectual enhancement literature is the most desirable source of pleasure. Whenever you feel low for some reason, pick up a good book from the shelf and immerse yourself in it. Literature comprises different genres. Whatever suits your taste and predilection you opt for it. And that will transport you to that world where you will have respite from the drudgery or discomfort you faced. Literature gives you pleasure and it entertains you. A good book is like a tonic that refreshes your mind. And mind is the storehouse of all our feelings and emotions that are associated with them. Your good habit of reading will influence your thoughts and views for bettering your personality. You technical expertise will earn you fame as long as you work. But your enlightened perception will develop your personality in such a way that it will make you welcome all the time at all places among anyone in the world.

Music also plays a part in developing our personality. You listen to some good music. Music soothes your ear and mind. Again here is a question of choice. You listen to the kind of music you like. Whether it is classical or modern is not important. It may be Indian classical that you have a fascination for. It may be western classical you like. It can be western pop or rock. It can be vocal or instrumental. It can be African tribal songs that fascinate you. The choice is absolutely yours. Whatever music it is you find it has a soothing effect when you either listen play or sing.

There are various genres of music. Similarly tastes and liking differ. Here we have to perceive and note that cultural influence affects greatly one's appreciation and fascination for music. Your predilection for music often is transmitted from the culture that prevails in your family. Whatever you have been listening to right from your childhood you might have cherished and that precisely has shaped your liking and interest. Of course it may get changed according to the environment and society that you experience while you are in college or in workplace. Your world is not confined to your family or home only. As you grow you enter a bigger world and that influences you in your thoughts and perceptions.

You were fond of Tagore's songs once. Now you listen to Hindi film songs. It is a matter of time and environment you are in. May be when you have come to another state where you do not listen to Tagore's songs you have grown a liking for the other forms of modern songs. But you still love music and that helps you to remain calm and free of pressure that you experience at your workplace.

Many of you possess the talent of composing poems and song. Indulging in creative work of art gives you immense satisfaction and when that finished work of art is appreciated by others you feel the joy of creation. Here the development of personality has two sides. One is the growth and development of aesthetic sense. You may not be an artist yourself. But your sense of appreciation will enable you to derive aesthetic pleasure from any artistic creation. Quite on the other hand if you are a creator then your sense of appreciation will enlarge your vision and you will admire and appreciate others' creativity as well. You as a person will make a mark by the dint of your encouraging and admiring spirit. Moreover the satisfaction that you derive by creating or composing is also there. You create and remain happy from within. Your sense of complacency will develop your emotional intelligence as well.

Personality is developed with the all round development of the mind. This can be obtained by observation of the well played roles of those characters in the performing arts. This explains why appreciation of literature and fine arts is imperative. Observation and interest in art, culture and literature deepens our perception and we imbibe many of our good qualities and shed some of the ones that we feel are shortfalls in the process. Keeping yourself engaged in good work also helps you in improving yourself and mind. Indulging in artistic pursuit helps improve and develop your personality in various ways. You save your leisure in utilizing it in a fruitful way. There are times when you have a tendency to spend your time uselessly. You really do not know what to do. May be you have some important assignments in hand. Yet you do not feel like doing it right then. What you can do is to do it later on and in the meantime you may either listen to music that you enjoy or read a book that gives you knowledge and pleasure.

Many among you may have the talent of creativity. You may have the potential of drawing and sketching. You have an excellent musical ear. You can pick up a tune that you hear being played in the music system. You hum it as it is sung and everybody appreciates your voice. Make it your pleasurable past time. You may take it up as a serious pursuit and you will soon realize that it gives you immense pleasure that will bring fulfilment in your life. A sense of completion makes a person inwardly happy and that provides him with satisfaction. A person who is happy and satisfied interacts with everyone well and is cheerful in disposition.

It will give you the impetus to work with a better mind and interact with others in a better way. This precisely is the impact on your personality. One of the key features of personality is cheerful disposition.

If you go through the biography of some of the great CEOs of reputed companies functioning across the world you will discover that they indulge in either some artistic activities or are lover and connoisseur of music or art. When life's activities become very demanding then one has to recourse to art, music and literature. That is the road to shirk the mind's pressure and get rest and tranquillity. It is a respite from the heavy schedule one goes through and that is a substitute to emotional balance.

If you go for formal training in music and later on pursue it as one of your passions it will help you in increasing your Intelligence as well. Music gives us the intelligent way to create and compose. Even emulating a singer or a rock star, calls for intelligence. You may have the talent but it needs proper application in order to reach the minimum level that is required. And that is how it helps you to be intelligent. The proper application of rhythm, melody and tune need to sync and make the rendition melodious. As a consequence you use your intelligent thinking in order to achieve that. On the whole it gives you pleasure, satisfaction and intelligence.

You listen to music if you feel you cannot sing or play a musical instrument. Music has no barrier and transcends all barriers. Whichever country you may belong to you can always develop a liking for music belonging to another part of the world. You are an Indian. Since childhood you have been only listening to modern songs belonging to Orissa. Now your profession has taken you to the USA. If you have a liking for music you will love to hear Michael Jackson or Pink Floyd if you so desire. The language is no barrier and neither the culture. In fact you benefit and remain happy since you do not cry over what you cannot get there.

If you love to sketch and draw you can do that even. An artist gets engrossed in his work of art and with a satisfied soul he accomplishes his work. His perseverance, patience and practice help him to reach his object. For the completion of his work he devotes himself entirely and dedicates his energy, enthusiasm and effort to create and complete his work. The prized qualities that he possesses help develop his personality too.

Not only that you have to be an artist to make yourself happy and satisfied. You can devote yourself to any other thing that you may have predilection for. You may enjoy gardening or do some social work to help the needy and the underprivileged.

In the current age of globalization we find identification crises causing concern to many. The steady growth of enterprise across the world has resulted in employees being relocated at cities and countries across the world. The cross cultural ambience thus created may be perceived as the root of crisis and conflict in the minds of people. The tremendous worry concerning recognition, growth and identification culminate in imbalance of mind. The employee who is an expatriate may face strong opposition in views and culture when away from home. Here what is needed is emotional intelligence to cope up with the situations that are beyond one's expectations.

To resolve any crises one needs to be dynamic and self oriented. There are various ways one can achieve that. Occupation and profession are not the same. The desire to do something that gives moral strength must be encouraged. We need to keep ourselves occupied mentally so that even if we are thousands of miles away from home we will not suffer from any conflict and crisis however intense it may appear.

DEVOTION AND DEDICATION

You may plant trees and water and nurture them to grow and maintain. One who has this inclination loves to watch a plant growing and the buds in them blossoming into beautiful flowers. To do any work with completion one needs to devote time and energy. If you decide to grow garden or plants you may do so. That will keep you occupied in your free and leisure time. Moreover that will give you joy and satisfaction. Especially when you see the plants bear flowers and fruits you feel the pleasure that cannot be obtained from any other source. It is the result of your hard work and devotion. The beautiful flowers in their riot of colours will be a feast for your eyes. You may rear a kitchen garden. That too will give you pleasure. The kitchen garden gives you vegetables some of which you eat and some you distribute to your friends. The pride of growing vegetables in your own garden is immense. When your garden produces vegetables you enjoy sharing them with your neighbours and friends. That is pleasurable for you. Gardening gives you joy and pleasure. It fosters in you devotion and dedication. Devotion to any work that you do gives you pleasure. If you extend your hand for a noble cause in society you will get satisfaction. Why will you do such a work? You will do that for the uplift of the underprivileged ones who are deprived from the simple privileges that life must offer them. Here too you need devotion. You cannot begin a work and leave it half way through. If you are dedicated to offer your service then you can choose from among the many options that are there. That may be in the form of literacy drive or organizing blood donation camp or any other social work for spreading awareness pertaining to health, hygiene or cleanliness. There are many areas where you can lend your helping hand for doing something for the need in your society. When you devote yourself to such selfless work you feel happy. You have satisfaction that you have done something to contribute to the society that you are in. The happiness that you experience is linked with your satisfaction that cannot be equated with material benefits that you reap from other work. This is an indication of a noble and generous mind in your person. Any selfless dedicated work like serving the society is noble. That sets example for others too.

One thing you must remember that this pleasure is something that cannot be obtained from any other material benefit that you get from other sources. To be more precise we enjoy and experience more pleasure when we work without any selfish motivation. And that is what one needs in order to have an inspiring personality.

COMMUNICATION AND ITS IMPACT ON PERSONALITY

It is a universal truth that cannot be denied that communication unfolds our personality. The way we talk, the way we deliver our speech, our selection of words and the intonation that accompanies our language – all reflect our personality. Good speakers are always known to create an impression and subsequently they become popular personalities. Your communication skill depends on certain parameters. They are:

Language: You can be a good communicator if you are able to convey your thoughts and ideas correctly and in appropriate language. There are two aspects. What are they?

The word 'correctly' refers to the correctness related to the syntax and grammar. Your expressions become correct by reading. While you read for enjoyment you pick up the language and acquire the required and necessary communicative style. Grammar and the rules of grammar are remembered not by learning but by listening and reading a text in the language where you come across the correct application of grammar throughout. That helps you indirectly to develop your sense of grammar. Moreover you find it much easier way of learning the technical aspects of language by reading. Reading keeps you enlightened besides brushing up your language skills. The latter you require for using it for communication. Communication skill is enhanced largely by reading as it enriches your vocabulary as well. While talking you do not get the time to think for the right word and expression. To be able to communicate effectively you need to express yourself in correct words. And this can be easily attained by extensive reading. Literature also makes you a man of taste. A well read person has a stunning personality because he develops the fine taste of speaking modestly, humorously and convincingly. All these are required for a person with great personality who talks impressively.

Vocabulary helps you in communicating with precision and correctness. If you read your vocabulary will increase and you will have no problem in communicating using the most appropriate and suitable words to express yourself clearly and spontaneously. When your vocabulary is enriched you can express your thoughts clearly without stammering or pausing for a word. This happens particularly with the language that is not your native tongue. English is not my native tongue. So when I use the language for communication I have to be sure that I get the right word while I speak. I know I can achieve that if I devote myself to reading extensively. Vocabulary helps me in speaking with correct expressions.

Communication has another salient feature that cannot be ignored. The manner and way of speaking plays a vital role. You may speak correct English or speak on any subject with clear perception and correct information. They help you to hone your expertise. Yet you need to develop yourself in some other areas as well. You should speak with articulation and with right intonation maintaining the emotional balance that actually depends on your emotional quotient. Whatever be your emotional state you need to maintain poise and grace while talking. That shows you are a good communicator. If you are to write anything then also you must be an adept in language. That helps you in writing effectively with the purpose you aim at. Both oral and written communications are important since a good communicator needs to possess the skill for speaking as well as writing. You will be endowed with an all round personality when you possess that.

How do you enrich your manner of speaking? Have you ever thought about it? You adopt the habit of speaking **articulately** and with proper **intonation**. Your confidence is conveyed through your clarity of expression and articulation. Whenever you are in a social gathering you speak with low volume lest you disturb others. But you must speak articulately.

Articulation is a mark of good communication and speech. When you talk you should make yourself clear and distinct enough for others to hear and understand you well. A person who speaks articulately is able to arrest the attention of his audience. Articulation establishes the fact that you are confident and certain of what you are speaking of. One who is not confident will try to speak rather rapidly to somehow complete what he wants to say. It is necessary for you adopt the habit of speaking articulately so that people know you have a bold personality.

A person known for a charming personality never forgets the **venue** he is in while he communicates. He talks courteously with everyone irrespective of the social standing of the person. His style of communication never varies. It is the same with everyone. Your manner of communication tells the audience or the recipient how much regard you have for that person. Here language plays an immensely important role. The same thing or idea can be spoken by three people in three different ways. Sometimes unknowingly one may hurt the sentiments of others. The speaker here may not have a sinister design of giving a blow to who he is communicating with but because he does not know the way he should speak he creates a negative impression in the minds of others.

Whether you are in an organization or not it is essential and proper for you to maintain the **decorum** while you communicate. Suppose you are talking to one of your colleagues and someone passes by who happens to be your colleague too you at least gesticulate to him in a sense of greeting to acknowledge his presence. If you do not do so then you seem to ignore him and that is not a mark of a good personality. Your communication and gestures are symbolic representations of your attitude and outlook. They are all interlinked and impact your personality. If you talk with courtesy and politely with all you will earn respect and deserve respect by all.

You find that some people have a bad habit of using slangs while talking. This is particularly so with those who are not well educated or literate. It is most improper for any person to use slangs while talking. For those who are uneducated or illiterate it may be overlooked. But for those who are educated and known for their education and profession or social background, it is significant. They need to be particular about this fact. It may be just out of habit that one uses slangs while being in the peer group with whom he may be very close and it becomes so ingrained in him that later on it becomes uncontrollable for that person to keep a check. He may find that unconsciously he has used some words out of mistake that are unacceptable in a genteel society. However if he speaks with extreme alertness while conversing he will be able to successfully avoid using any undesirable and unacceptable words while talking. As we see everything depends on the person's desire and will. Ultimately it is your mind and thought processes that need to be regulated and controlled. You will have no problem in maintaining the decorum that is expected from you.

In this context we need to remember another point. It is the use of **humour**. Often we try to be humorous while communicating. However to use wit and humour in your conversation you need to adhere to proper sense of the words and meaning your humour conveys. While being humorous you should be careful in not hurting the sentiments of others. I happen to know a college teacher who holds an honourable post in the college. He often tries to be humorous without having the slightest regard for his colleague's sentiment. The language he uses or the subject he broaches are often not respectable. He forgets the venue and the people he is talking to. All of us do not have the ability to humour with a graceful taste. We need to remember that there is a wide difference between cheap jokes and humour. That is why one should be careful in what one says to others. Humour undoubtedly adds flavour to your talk provided you have a deep insight into the matter you mention.

Literature unfolds to us a gamut of technical devices. Humour is one of them. Many eminent writers are known for their excellence in bringing humour in their writing that adorns their creativity.

There is another important area that we need to consider while communicating. The forum where we converse is significant in the sense we need to follow the **protocol** of communication that the forum demands. Organizational communication involves too much of intricacies at certain levels. So while communicating in an organization you ought to consider the intricacies involved according to the situation and persons with whom you are conversing. Suppose you are the in-charge of a department and there are around forty people working under you. You interact with them from time to time. When you hold a conversation with one of your junior employees you may dictate and command according to the task you intend to assign. However your way of conversation has an effect. You have your prerogatives and privileges to use the chain of commands by virtue of your hierarchical position. While giving your commands you choose a suitable style of communicative mode. Several features of you as a person come out while you communicate with others. You remember this always. You decide the best way to communicate with whoever you have to communicate. Of course it cannot be the same with respect to everyone. Some aspects of your communication will undergo variation while you keep in view the hierarchical position of the person concerned. That may be the linguistic style or expressions. When you communicate with someone belonging to an upper hierarchy you use some words that you may easily do away with while communicating with someone who belongs to your level or to a lower level. With your boss or anyone belonging to the upper hierarchy the style may be different. It may be, on the other hand another style when you communicate with someone belonging to lower hierarchy. Style obviously includes intonation and language used for communication. So we see even in the same venue we speak in different ways maintaining the protocol of the venue.

Again in different places or in different venues your **style** of communication may assume different forms. At home you talk to your siblings in a way that you don't do with your neighbours. Here comes a question of proximity. With someone whom you share a close relationship you may be absolutely informal in your style and manner of communication. You can be friendly and use the endearing terms that are not all appropriate for you to use when you communicate with someone who is not so close to you.

Control with your voice is a must. You should be attentive to the **volume** of your speech. Especially when you are in a public forum you should talk to your acquaintances in a soft tone. It should not be loud enough to catch others' attention. Moreover speaking aloud in a public forum is not a sign of decency. Here mannerisms and decorum matter. An individual with a proper sense of manner does not talk loudly unless and until it is emergency or absolutely essential. The volume, the style and the intonation of the language you are speaking proclaim the person you are.

Intonation is the sound that emits as you speak. Intonation reflects our personality. You can differentiate the background of one individual with that of the other by listening to the intonation of each one of them. It is absolutely essential for you to use the right intonation of the language you speak. Intonation makes a mark of difference. You can classify someone from the perspective of social class and background by the intonation of the person. From the intonation of someone speaking English you can make out whether that speaker is used to speak English or not.

You speak in a decent way with all around you and when it is time for you to **listen**, you listen carefully. Listening patiently and attentively is a rare quality of a person. One who listens carefully is a man with great personality. You must have seen that people while communicating hardly care to listen to attentively to the ones they are communicating with. This is a common phenomenon that affects the communication process and shoots ill consequences too. Imagine you are talking to someone and he/she does not pay attention to all that you say. How do you feel in that case? Surely you feel less interested in communicating with that person. Here the recipient of your communication exposes himself/ herself as a person with a careless attitude. There is an interesting example that can be given. A teacher enters the classroom and says something that some of the students do not listen to. Some students listen to and responds to all that she says. The teacher's impression here is twofold. The group comprising students who listen to are regarded as individuals with decorum and she respects their values. Whereas the ones who are busy in gossiping from time to time with their neighbours are regarded as unmannerly and devoid of their sense of decorum. Here the classification of personality traits are made on the basis of their behavioural attitude as revealed in their role played in listening.

In an organization as a leader you must cultivate the habit of listening. You need to be a patient listener when any of your colleagues comes and talks of a problem. You need to listen to him carefully in order to understand his problem. That will enable you to solve the problem that he faces for which he has come to you to seek help. Besides that his regard for you will double when he discovers that you listen minutely to all that he says. In a meeting you are chairing it is not that you are speaking throughout. There are other speakers too who speak. And you have to listen. Important discussion entails proper listening and comprehending. The conclusion or inference on the basis of discussion can be arrived at if one listens to the entire discussion with care and attentive mind.

Have you observed how doctors listen to their patients? They do it carefully. They need to because they cannot diagnose properly or treat their patients carefully if they do not listen. There is another side to the coin. If a doctor does not listen to his patients he creates a very negative image and the patients dislike this attitude of the doctor.

Another example will make the case more obvious. In a group people are talking. Strangely enough one of them is only willing to impose her views on others. She does not give chance to others to speak. Even when others are speaking she talks in between without listening to others. That is annoying as well as unmannerly. Allowing others to speak and listening to others is a courteous gesture.

Communication includes non-verbal cues as well. Here when I talk about communication I imply the non-verbal cues too. The **proximity** that you maintain while communicating is important. The distance you maintain while talking to someone shows your position and relationship with that person. We do not have the same kind of nearness with everybody. Naturally we have to be careful specially while talking or communicating.

While communicating orally we make movements of our hands and head. That is we use **gestures** to convey our message. It is a natural and spontaneous movement of hands and body. However you must have noticed that gestures differ widely from person to person. And there we have to take note of one salient feature. Gestures are spontaneous and they are accompanied by the conversations that we make. But often our gestures are overdone in the sense that we make too much of hand movements to impart our message. That may have an effect on the mind of our audience. Either the attention is drawn towards the movement of the hands or the speaker seems very cumbersome. It is wise to make a modest movement of hands so that we do not appear awkward to the audience. And the audience is able to attend to what we say when we make less of hand and body movements.

Posture also contributes to the non-verbal communication that reflects one's personality. You see so many people walking down the road. Or perhaps you see someone sitting in the passengers' waiting lounge at the airport. You may not know him but from the sitting posture of the passenger you form an impression that reveals his personality. A person who comes from a respectable background has a proper sitting posture that is quite conspicuous from the manner of his sitting. The way a person stands, the way a person sits are a reflection of the person's personality. On the other hand you also happen to see people in the same venue with an odd sitting posture. It is very awkward to see people lifting up their legs in the couch they are sitting forgetting entirely where they are. Their point of view perhaps is they are waiting comfortably and what is it to anybody? The place is meant for their comfort. They give you an impression that they are sitting and enjoying the company of their friends in their drawingroom. Such postures bear an impression that cannot be considered with regard and respect. It only proves the person to have a weak personality who does not maintain proper decorum in relation to postures in a public place. At home we may sit in the manner we like. It is because that place is meant for our comfort. But in the office or in the place where we work we should maintain proper standing and sitting postures. Even in a public forum we should care for these details. Postures indicate the persons we are. Hence it is something we cannot afford to neglect.

There is another important aspect in relation to postures. As a professional you may have to give a presentation. When you address a group of audience you stand in a proper posture so that it enhances your personality. You captivate your audience by your smart appearance and standing posture. Remember the audience who may be listening to you for the first time will assess your personality by your first appearance on the stage. Your gait and your standing posture and the way you greet the audience will indicate your personality. Stand straight while you talk. Your smile and cheerful disposition will earn a place in the hearts of your audience. That is the first indicator of your personality. Your courage and strength of personality is revealed in the way you stand and face the audience. Your audience will look at you as you enter the stage. When you begin to speak and address them they become attentive to your speech and judge your speaking skill. Then will follow the knowledge and depth of your subject matter that is counted later on. Your manner of speaking will tell them whether you are confident or not. Of course when you come to the stage and make your appearance it will be obvious if you are confident. Your nervousness on the other hand makes you look shaky. That is reflected in your manner of walking and standing posture. So, to avoid being seen as a nervous person, try to gain confidence and develop a sense of positivity. Think positively that you will be able to perform your task well and proceed on. You will walk boldly and smartly without feeling nervous in front of the audience who are closely noticing you.

In the interview venue some students feel so nervous that they may stagger and enter. The interviewee is noted right from the time they enter. Your posture, gait and etiquette are important. You sit properly and do not reveal your nervousness by either tapping on the table or making odd movements of body and hands. Even for group discussion you follow the norms of proper sitting postures to maintain decorum as well as demonstrate your boldness and confidence.

The position of legs is also important when you sit along with others in a formal gathering. That includes both your sitting posture and your manner of placing the legs. There are no hard rules to follow. What you need is proper sitting posture to create a good impression. In your workplace you have to be alert how you sit as anybody may come to meet you and talk to you. You cannot keep your legs stretched right across the table even if you feel like doing so. Whenever we go to anyone's house we follow the decorum related to postures. The way we sit, walk and stand show the person in us. Have you observed that sitting postures are closely associated with the various occupations and vocations people are involved in?

The singers or other performing artists have their definite postures and movements on stage while they perform. So do the teachers when they teach in the lecture hall. In fact postures differ with the kind of profession one is in.

In this context we must remember one thing. We see people belonging to different parts of the world have different perception. You might have noticed that the cultural practice or may be the attitude one has belonging to one place varies so widely with the others that it seems unfathomable how those people live together or stay together. Yet people live in unity in spite of diversity. This is so because man is a social being and loves to think that everybody likes him. He has the power to adjust and accommodate in diverse situations and environment.

This is the uniqueness in man that prompts him to develop his personality so that he is appreciated, liked and admired. This also makes him become famous and popular. Talent and potentials help an individual achieve an outstanding feat. But when such a person is endowed with the desirable elements of personality that are worshipped by others he/she becomes an icon.

Even if one is a celebrity it is not always that one is looked upon as an impressive personality. Among his/her intimate circle he/she may not have the kind of popularity one dreams of, the reason being his/her not so amiable a disposition. May be the person suffers from too much of vanity or feelings of superiority.

Obviously that celebrity will not attain popularity as a person. People will like him and respect him for the special attribute he possesses to become a celebrity. Personality however includes some other attributes or traits like humility or modesty that one may be lacking. And vanity or ego will deprive a person of the love and respect that common man would have had for him.

When we talk about celebrities the name of Amitabh Bacchan comes to our mind as a charismatic personality. There are a number of film stars who may be great actors and have won reputation in their domain for excellent and outstanding achievement. Yet when we compare them with Amitabh Bachhan we are likely to infer that the latter is the most charming personality. When we think deeply we will come to the conclusion that he possesses those elements of personality that captivate his admirers all over.

The industrial tycoons, the film stars, great musicians or prodigies who make a great impact by their outstanding feats are not necessarily the persons with extraordinary personality. The ones who are extraordinarily talented and enjoy a glorious name and fame are known for their excellent accomplishments in life. Their greatness lies in the fact that they are achievers. That also makes them great personalities in the sense all of them possess certain attributes of impressive personalities like discipline, punctuality, tenacity, patience etc. to be able to reach excellence in that special field. That creates the enigmatic impression in the minds of their fans.

Be that as it is the celebrities are the ones who have already made their mark as great persons and we can always get inspiration from their achievements. They have some key features of personality in them to make them so successful. Looking at it from this point of view we should observe the quality that he /she owns that has made him/her so great a person. It is that aspect of his/her personality that deserves respect and everybody feels the charm that is there. Another important thing is that a celebrity has an occupation that gives inspiration to work with dedication and devotion.

It is quite a different story for the others who do not belong to this group. But for that matter we cannot say that we are not capable of ennobling ourselves with the visions of doing something to achieve satisfaction in life. In fact we too can be achievers in our own way. Whatever I do in life if I devote myself entirely to the work and put in my effort I will surely achieve my goal. However minor the work may be I will be happy and contented and feel delighted. Satisfaction enhances our peace and joy. That feel is something that we all crave for.

For individuals who are professionals or entrepreneurs it is important to develop those features that they have inherited and possess so that they become more admirable and respectable in society. By developing those features they evince love and admiration from others. Besides their person will be a source of inspiration for others as well.

Personality development starts from very early stages of life. Interestingly as parents and teachers we can try to inculcate some of these features in them. Apart from the basic sense of ethics and morals we can also guide them in building up positive views in everything they do. Children and teenagers need proper guidance. If we have the alertness and desire to bring up our future generations properly we can set examples by developing our personality.

Whether we are professionals or entrepreneurs we must try to sharpen our various features of personality that will be influential for our children. We know what the key features of personality are. Accordingly we can endeavour so that we better our personality and earn respect and admiration from all around us. Trying to achieve our objective with persistent effort is something that hones our personality.

Students and teenagers who learn from us should be treated with sympathy and love. They often are prompted by emotions and jump to an action without a forethought. This creates an impact on their minds. Sometimes emotional upsurge results in evil consequences. Often they get influenced by what they see in the films and entertainment medium. They need emotional balance and emotional intelligence to judge everything from a proper perspective.

Not only the young generation, the old and the aged ones in the family sometimes become emotional maniacs. They react beyond proportion when they suffer from emotional crisis. They become so sensitive that it is difficult for them to bear the pain at the slightest. It creates problem for others as well. Hence it is necessary for everyone to try to develop their emotional intelligence so that they can lead their lives happily and peacefully.

Emotional intelligence helps in developing our other skills as well. We become more adept in communication and understand the limits of conversation, the nuances of body language that assist in gauzing the personality of an individual.

4

Values and Ethics

Practice of Self discipline and soft skills that help in Emotional Intelligence

Art and culture speak volumes of a nation. A connoisseur of painting can easily tell you the quintessence of any masterpiece hanging in the picture gallery of a museum. The artist, the painter or a sculptor delineate the various aspects of the world we live in. We as beholder enjoy and admire. We also glean information and it illumines our mind. A person develops his mind and fine sense of appreciation through the cultivation of art, painting or sculpting. And that influences his/her personality. In other words an individual whets his soft skills while creating or indulging in the fine arts. That disciplines an artist's mind as well. Any artistic pursuit is a deep meditation. One pursues one's art with passion and tenacity. The regularity involved in practice and creating makes one self-disciplined. The object of an artist's passion is to reach the level of excellence. He/she has to work and persevere hard in order to attain that. However talented one is there cannot be any alternative for hard work. One achieves success by disciplined and assiduous cultivation of the artistic pursuit one has in mind.

Persistent struggle to reach one's objective is what is required in order to achieve success. This helps one to become successful in the pursuit of his objective. The desire and aspiration motivates you but in order to attain your desired object you need to have perseverance, self-discipline and tenacity. An artist who is endowed with artistic passion possesses these elements to reach his goal. And that makes an artist renowned and known. To achieve your mission successfully you need to be self-disciplined like an artist. You may belong to any profession. But your self-discipline helps you climb the ladder of success and reach the pinnacle of glory.

Soft skills teach us several important things besides the way to communicate. What are soft skills? Soft skills is a package that lends you support in developing those skills that are complementary to your technical skills. They are the ones that provide you with the touch that is required for developing your personality. Let us discuss those elements that are components of soft skills. Your soft skills help you to flower your talent and to become a successful artist.

Etiquette is one of the most important elements in developing your soft skills. You may be very sound technically. Your knowledge pertaining to your work and domain area may be sound. You are well read person in your field and there is hardly any person who can be at par with you so far as your knowledge and expertise is concerned. Everyone praises you and has a high notion of your competence in the work you do. Yet you are not able to hold the endearing place in your employer or your colleagues. They are inwardly not happy with you. The reason is you do not follow etiquette. Consciously or unconsciously you seem to avoid the etiquette that is demanded in an interface with the officials. You have never paid any attention to this. Nor will you in future. But it has a negative impact on everyone's mind. Their impression about you is not pleasant so far as your behaviour is concerned.

There are nuances of etiquette that you ought to follow. You have to wish the officials when you meet them in the morning as you reach your office. Saying 'Good Morning' to your colleagues or the officials is something you cannot afford to omit. There should not be any slip on your part. Your sense of etiquette is a reflection of your personality. Asking someone 'How do you do?' or saying 'Good Morning' does not cost you anything. It pays back in return. When someone has done a favour to you, you express your thankfulness to the person for obliging you. Any request granted by someone should not go unnoticed. A gesture of thanks is what etiquette demands. Expressing your gratitude for any obligation you receive shows that you are full of etiquette.

Think from your perspective. Suppose you go to meet someone for an official purpose. His PA takes your V card and you are called after a wait for a minute or so. You enter the gentleman's cabin and say: 'Good Morning'. There is no smile in his face, nor does he say anything just nods his head. You wait for him to ask you to take your seat. Since he does not, you yourself drag the chair in front and decide to sit. Imagine a situation like this. How would you have felt? May be the work for which you have gone is done and you are contented. Yet you have something bugging you. To you that gentleman has absolutely no sense of etiquette. And you know he is an MD of an organization. All these reflect his personality and you form an ill notion against him as a person without etiquette. Everyone whose personality is respectable possesses good manners and etiquette. That explains why you need to practise proper etiquette and manners in order to develop your personality to make it an impressive one.

Many things appear trivial and insignificant to us. We do not attach much importance to them while in our interactive interface. We ignore and overlook something that unknowingly cost us in the long run. Subtle details that we ignore if considered would have paid us dividends. Like, you reply a mail immediately you receive it. There may be some who do not care to answer a mail that has been received. Or even if one answers it one does it with tardiness. But this is not brooked by the ones who are punctual and meticulous about all these details. Especially in an organization where you see your colleagues and the coworkers are prompt enough to follow the etiquette you pose yourself as a person indicating a negative view. How can you then expect to be the one with a personality to be remembered for the virtues you have? Rather people will know you as a person who lack in punctuality and etiquette.

Style and manner are also important. That elevates your personality. Your manner of talking, manner of walking (gait) and manner of carrying yourself are some of the salient components of soft skills. They together constitute your personality. Hence it is essential for you to consider them as areas to be improved and attach importance as well. Someone extremely decorous and with gentle manners is indeed a pleasant personality. You have only to question yourself: 'Am I like that?' And you get your answer. If you are not you can always try and become so. All of us are not beautiful to look at. There we are bound by limitations. But all of us can have good manners and style to interact with everyone beautifully. That is how we can become a good person and impress others to be like us if they are not so.

Appearance and looks: All of us are not blessed with handsome features and beautiful looks. But all of us can make our appearance smart and impressive. Appearance includes your looks. As I have already mentioned we need not consider our eyes or nose when we think of our looks. We are born with the look that we get from our genes. Whether I am dark or fair, short or tall, possess brown eyes or black ones cannot be helped. We cannot alter them. Exceptions are of course there for the ones who would like to do so because their look may affect their profession. Those are the exceptions and exceptions cannot be the rule however. We belong to the common range where we have to be contented with our inherited looks that cannot be changed. Contentment makes you happy and to pine for what you have not got will only make you unhappy.

But here we are not concerned with the 'looks' that we mean while we talk of someone being beautiful and pretty or someone being very plain looking. For developing your personality you do not need to be beautiful and handsome. It is the looks that enhances our inner beauty that we talk of. The inner beauty of a person develops his personality. How can we possess inner beauty? Of course by being emotionally and spiritually intelligent we all become beautiful. Our inner stability and restraint endow us with the beauty we are talking of. Restraint is quite challenging a task to begin with. There are so many provocations and temptations you find all around that it requires a strong will power and determination to stay away and stabilize the mind when it dwindles at them. Your realization that the provocations and temptations will not lead to anything permanent will make you stay away from them.

It is then that you will grow beautiful from within. There will be no ill feelings or negative thoughts to disturb your mind. You will neither be envious of anybody nor will you be vain and arrogant. You will look more beautiful than the ones among us whom we regard as beautiful because of their features and physical beauty that is absolutely external. You will surpass them with your inner beauty and you will be respected for that.

In this context I would like to mention that great saints and sages of all times impress thousands of people by their deed and work. They impress people by their inner beauty, intrepidity and courage. This is evident that we must have a bold appearance and positive look in order to develop our personality. And the very thought that lingers in our mind that we need to be beautiful like sculptor's art if we have to have charismatic personality is incorrect.

Neat appearance is something that adds to your personality. Wherever you go you need to go wearing dresses that are neat and clean. Cleanliness includes your mane and how you maintain them. Combing your hair properly is not adequate enough. You must have a proper haircut especially when you go for any interview, any formal gathering, or any business meeting. Appearance creates an impression that can have a long lasting effect. For ladies too it is important to dress properly befitting the situation and profession they are in. These are important parameters to create an impression that adds up to one's personality.

Smartness has nothing to do with the outfit you adorn yourself with. Smartness comes with your appearance and the confidence with which you interact with others. In other words your smartness is more related to your inner self than your outer appearance. Your confidence, your boldness, your honesty will help you to become smart. Once you are endowed with these you become smart and your appearance will be impressive.

We often relate smartness with the characters in the fiction. They are portrayed as smart robbers or gangsters involved in criminal offence. Their smart escapades attract the viewers and readers. They move around with a smart appearance imprinted on everybody's mind. But would you call them inspiring?

They are not true selves. They are exaggerated versions or caricatures. Hence we can never go by their examples. Though they do not lead a path of righteousness they hold their head high without the slightest scruple. Their intellect is never challenged. Such characters have their place in the realm of fiction only. Astoundingly they have no place in the world we move around. Had it been so criminals and social miscreants would have respectfully led their lives. But they dominate the underworld knowing fully well that they are scorned by the society. And they have their subdued feelings of agony blended with fear for the sinful life they lead. Their personality bears the trait of a psychopath.

As a matter of fact there are many saintly characters in reality whom we can cite as examples of an epitome of smartness. They are bold and courageous because they have no inhibitions that stem from dishonesty and falsehood. They are smart in the true sense of the term. Smartness refers to those who can speak boldly, walk with firm steps without fear and doubt. They are endowed with the fine traits of personality like patience, endurance, love and intrepidity that are inspiring for all.

In our earlier discussion we have touched upon the role played by values and ethics in our personality development. We know values are mostly imbibed from family, community and religious belief one has. By and large we have observed that people with a deep religious bent of mind are sometimes inclined to think and judge from a religious perspective. That is, they value some major aspects of life from the point of view of what religion has fostered in them. You feel that consuming animal flesh is highly improper because your religion has taught you to abstain from it. And you have grown up with that belief since your school days. But when you come to the college and on a joyous occasion when your friend is throwing a party you are astounded to see chicken or beef or beer. What is your immediate reaction? It is almost like Adam's experience whether to taste the forbidden fruit or not. It is your values' strength that holds you back. If you yield that shows you have a different take on the matter. It is either a weakness on your part or your change of perception that has simultaneously changed your values as well. So in both ways you see values play a distinct part in personality of an individual.

Religion is often associated with observations of rituals. Here what is interesting to note is that in India we have so many religious beliefs prevailing that values are reflected in the personality quite deeply. It should be taken as general observation and not case specific. Early risers often are prompted by the thought that waking up early and praying will benefit them, as prayers purify the souls and help us to do our deed in the right way. There can be number of examples stated that will go to prove that rigidity and flexibility of attitudes and prejudices depend largely on the religious views one attaches oneself to. They shape our personality in the like manner.

We are inclined spiritually if we have such associations in life. Many of us are successful professionals and we may have spiritual bent of mind. This is not merely being religious in the way of performing ritualistic rites accompanied with religion. Spiritual bent of mind develops our personality in more ways than one. The essence of spiritual inclination directs us to righteous path and helps us to realize the truth and goal of life. In the process we change ourselves for attaining that goal. And simultaneously our personality is developed. With an enlightened mind we are able to relinquish those human propensities that curb our way to sublimity. The realization that our glorious deeds like adhering to honesty in the profession is everything emerges from within. It actually helps in the growth of our personality. No outward force has such strength to elevate our thoughts and mind. Of course we get influences from some sources like books, religious and moral instructions imbibed from school and parents and also from the environment in which we are brought up.

But when some impositions come from outside you find there is in several cases an opposing force working. That may obstruct and oppose all that are enforced and imposed upon. So it is better you be positive about all that you do in life. If you have positive view and notion about the work you are to embark on you will gain confidence and courage. Positive thinking helps you a lot. I give an example that will establish the truth of the matter.

A girl was to give a solo performance on stage. She was extremely talented and practised thoroughly the song she was going to play in guitar. However she had a negative thought that she would not be able to perform well, constantly plaguing her. She reached the venue well before time. When she got up on the stage panic gripped her. She felt so nervous to see such a big audience. And she could not perform as well as she hoped for. Her teacher too was there to notice that she was pretty nervous. That marred her performance. Of course she played well but it was not outstanding that she deserved. This explains why we need to be positive in our attitude and visions. Our positive attitude guides us to go ahead and perform excellently.

Positive attitude gives you strength, desire to work and perseverance to proceed with your work. Even if you suffer from disappointment at any point in the middle of your project you derive inspiration from the positive attitude. That acts as a drive and empowers you to carry on with zest and energy. If you go through the biography of any renowned person who is an achiever you will find that he or she must have had positive attitude throughout that had been the source of inspiration for him or her in the midst of all odds. It is not unusual for an individual to go through a phase of disappointment or frustration at one point of life however successful he may be. During that phase his moral support is derived from all the positive attitudes he has. That in fact boosts up his spirit in times of crisis and problem. That also helps him to enhance his emotional control and restraint.

If we take help from such examples we benefit and learn how to have positive attitude to everything we do in life and that actually develops our personality.

Values and ethics that we imbibe from literature

Literature unfolds a gamut of incidents and characters. They are the writer's creation. At the same time they are the replica of human beings we see or hear about in our lives. We often identify the characters, their behaviour, attitude or personality with those around us. There is no mistaken identity that is wrapped under the guise of fictitious name. They can be identified as someone who we know. Impossibility does not reign in literature. When you read Lev Tolstoy's *Resurrection* you identify the protagonist's vices and his sense of guilt that makes him take a very bold step of marrying a prisoner. Once you identify the virtues and vices portrayed in the story you play the role of a judge. The judge knows what is evil, what is immoral, what is right or what is wrong. This knowledge helps in awakening our consciousness. Values are given a strong foothold in literature. The appeal of good literature lies in the fact that it has a lingering effect on the mind. That is why it makes you think and contemplate. And you are able to analyze and perceive the truth and reality from various dimensions.

What the historians narrate or social reformers say is to let people know facts that are taking place. But what the writer says in the form of literary art is for people to perceive and think. Such is the effect of literature. It creates or changes values and perception. The age-old maxim 'The pen is mightier than sword' is undoubtedly true. The values that we have are strengthened by the ones that literature fosters on us.

Ethics guard us from doing anything immoral and offensive. Ethics help us to stay away from sinful acts. Persons with proper ethics can never do what is undesirable.

In this context I may refer to some examples I come across while I interact with my students while taking the class. I distinctly remember the discussion I had with my students while narrating the importance of ethics in business. The students were quite vociferous in opining that it is irrelevant and impossible a term associated with business. And then one of the students cited an example of how a chemist shopowner sells medicine without giving the cash receipt to his customers as it remains unaccounted for and it exempts him from paying the taxes of the sales he made, adding that even the customers also accept this since they are made to pay less for the drugs they buy. Well this may be a stray incident. But you must keep in mind that if one becomes unethical as an entrepreneur or as a professional working in others' organization then he encourages corruption and that ultimately leads to punishable offence for which the perpetrator of unethical deeds will have to face the ill consequences. Any person from top to bottom should have proper values and sense of ethics. I have already discussed this point.

What is very important for you to remember as an ethical person is that personalities like you will be instrumental in developing an organization and a nation. The good will of a company comes from the social responsibility the company bears. Our sense of commitment generates from our responsibility and goodwill we cherish. All these are interlinked with our ethics. The common idea that we harbour very wrongly is that no businessman is ethical. That is a wrong supposition. What happens is that we have a tendency to generalize on the basis of few incidents that we come across. Even the bureaucrats who are steering the country's administration need to be ethical. If we want persons with praiseworthy personalities then we should remember that ethics that inspires us to be truthful and honest should be adhered to, in every instance.

Ethics encourages us to be committed and honest in our commitment. Throughout our life we make so many promises and think of fulfilling them. But sometimes we give false promises and go back on our words. That is improper and not encouraging at all. You often come across people who say that they will do a certain thing within a time. But when the time arrives they are not to be traced anywhere. And perhaps do not do the work at all. This is an example of a false promise that one gives. If you promise anything to anyone you must think beforehand whether you will be able to execute the job timely or not. Then only you commit that you will do it. If you make a promise you must follow it strictly so that you do not have to break your promise. It is not a good practice to go on giving false hopes. If you are not certain of your competence then it is wise not to take the onus of doing anything that is beyond your capability. Often we think if we say 'I will do this surely by tomorrow' I will be regarded as a responsible person and a competent one. But when we fail to keep our promise we prove to be not only incompetent but an irresponsible liar. So it is essential for us to follow a path of honesty so far as the personality is concerned. Making promises and going back on those words is not proper for any professional who enjoys a reputed social status.

To earn respect you have to prove your worth and exhibit your deserving attributes. You promise whatever you can execute according to your ability. You should always be keen on completing your work well before time. If you are in the habit of keeping things pending then you will find you have still piles of work heaped upon them. That will only mess up your work and you will not be able to finish them satisfactorily. Whether it is your personal work or official work you must do it timely to prove yourself an honourable person who keeps his promises.

HEALTH AND MIND

We are inured to the pressures of life so intensely that we crave for a little respite from it. The respite is needed for both health and mind.

To practise control and restraint we need strong determination and will. That is the first step that we go through when we plan to improve our mind and body. The resolution that we make helps us achieve our targeted goals. You need strength of mind to help improve your mind. Yoga and meditation help you to attain that seemingly impossible goal. Meditation makes your mind calm and quiet. Our mind seems to jostle with ongoing and continuous thought processes. We can hardly stop thinking when we are awake. Whether those thoughts are constructive or not that is a question to be considered. Be that as it may they often are there to distract our mind from the focus of attention. You may have noticed that occasionally while studying a chapter that you have to prepare for your examination you get distracted time and again. And however much you try you find that you are not able to bring your mind to the chapter. You may be constantly reminded of some comments by one of your classmates during the class. Or you get flashes of visions evoked by the moments spent with your friends a few hours ago. All these create a world of silent movie in your mind like a kaleidoscope. To get rid of this state requires exercise of mind. That can come through meditation.

By meditation I do not mean spirituality or religious practices. What meditation refers to is bringing the focus of consciousness to a point by obliterating the thoughts that our mind is occupied with. Initially meditation seems a difficult task. It is indeed a hard job to bring down the focus of consciousness to one point even for a fraction of a minute. Determined efforts prove helpful. Our persistent effort helps us to achieve the goal. The procedure may be time consuming. You have to be patient in order to make yourself attuned to the ambience. For meditation choose a place that is preferably away from noise. Sit on the floor and keeping your eyes closed gradually narrow down your mind to a point. The moment that you stay like that may be a few seconds. Try it the next day. The next day you will find you can at least bring your mind to the point of concentration with ease. May be the time you can stay with your focus of concentration will be no more than you did the day before. However you should not give it up. This may continue for some days. After a passage of time you will find that you can concentrate well for a longer time. Thus you can begin meditation in a proper way. Meditation will regulate your mind to your benefit. The mind that was beyond control erstwhile will gradually become your slave. You will see that you are able to concentrate better. The wonderful effect of meditation is, it makes one calm and serene. The mind in its state of serenity stays unaffected by the turbulence of events that take place outside. Once your mind is trained, no outward force will revert it to its erstwhile state.

As you learn to meditate you will realize the value of self-discipline and you will monitor your activities judiciously by adhering to discipline. Discipline helps us to achieve success in whatever we undertake to do.

Discipline is what we learn from our childhood. Yet many of us do not lead a disciplined life. Discipline refers to habits as well. The maintenance of time in relation to our daily chores and work is the first step of discipline. If you follow discipline then you will find you are able to do your work more efficiently than others. A person who is disciplined finds time to do his work well and gets the energy to do his work successfully.

A child learns discipline from school. It cannot do as it wishes in the classroom and has to conform to all the regulations that are there. Here a child goes by the strictness adhered to the disciplinary actions. May be fear of punishment makes it do as it ought to do. It knows if it does not go by the rules that it is supposed to follow it will be punished. Perhaps this imposition of rules makes it disciplined. In a way it is good. But at home if the child is allowed to do whatever it wants then it will not really understand the value of discipline and it will definitely be not disciplined in the true sense of the term. So the parents too, have a part to play to teach discipline to their children.

Discipline makes one regular and punctual. The disciplined person knows what should be done when and where. In the classroom the students are asked not to make a noise. The reason is to create an ambience that would help the class to go on undisturbed.

If a student is encouraged or demonstrated to sit quietly for sometime without any physical movement and making no noise then the student will gradually pick up the habit. Later on he will learn to meditate.

That will help him to acquire the required elements to develop his personality. Meditation allows one to stay detached from the mundane realities and become more objective while perceiving a situation.

Discipline helps in developing other areas of personality as well. All our prejudiced views take birth from the inhibitions that cloud our mind. Our mind becomes crystal clear when we become absolutely stable both physically and mentally. The latter is possible through meditation. Stability of mind gives us time enough to think of anything clearly and objectively. In a hurry we often judge and view things swayed by emotions and impulses. This can best be explained when we overreact with our children' failure or obstinacy. We should ourselves be disciplined enough to be able to transmit it to our children or students.

A child needs to be handled delicately. We the adults are responsible for inculcating the right values to a child or a youth. The communication or soft skills have a pivotal role to play. We must talk to our children politely and refrain from scolding them. When we talk about self-discipline we need to scan the areas that come under this category.

Regularity: Right from our childhood we should follow and observe regularity in whatever we do. Regularity affects both our health and mind. Regularity refers to doing any work on a particular time at regular intervals. Starting from morning till night we need to be regular in doing the work we do. This develops the sense of being regular in any activity we are involved in. When we do anything regularly we achieve success. Regularity helps us to achieve our objective. This can best be illustrated by the little participants contesting in the music competition aired in the reality shows nowadays. The young and small kids are able to accomplish their objective by maintaining regularity. They are made to practise regularly and that boosts up their inner potential. Because they are participating in the competition they have to practice and the show continues for about seven to eight months at a stretch. The regularity they perforce maintain makes them realize the value of regularity right from this age. They themselves see the effect of their regular practice and effort put up together. They become gradually better performers as the judges comment on their performance. And day by day they show remarkable improvements. That develops their personality too. A person who maintains regularity is able to achieve good results in his effort.

It goes with respect to health as well. One should follow a regular pattern for having food, bath, sleep and exercise. If you decide to get up 6o'clock in the morning then do that regularly. It should not be like getting up at six one day, seven the next day and eight on another day. Of course out of three sixty five days one or two days you may break the regularity when perhaps you may have a problem related to health or time schedule. But regularity with time in relation to health, food and other physical and mental activities should be maintained.

A regular diet keeps you fit and healthy. Eating habits need to be regular and controlled. Consumption of food irregularly has an adverse impact on health. If you remain healthy you will be physically fit and look smart. Smartness in turn adds to your personality. You move around doing your work efficiently because your good health permits you to do so. You never feel lazy and sloth. Regularity includes the cleanliness of your body too. Regular bath and cleanliness of body keeps you in good health and mind as well.

Thus we see regularity keeps all of us in sound health and mind. Regularity is a must in everything we do. When we are students we need to be regular in our studies. If we feel we will do that just before the exam we will not be able to do so. There are two sides to it. When you study regularly your brain is having an intellectual exercise that whets your memory, analytical power and comprehension. But when we choose to do the work for a certain period of time like just before the exam for instance, you will find you take more time to understand the fact, more time to retain the facts that you learn and you will not be prompt in applying the knowledge that you obtain, as you would have done had you been regular in your studies. Your brain requires regular exercise of mind and intellect to be alert and sound.

If you do your work regularly on time then you would not have to over work in any circumstances. That will help you and save you from being pressurized and tensed under various circumstances. You will not feel the tension of work that has not been done. If you have work pending then that will affect both your mind and body. The mind will be too occupied with pressure of time and completing the work that is not yet done. And when you try to finish the work completely and overstrain yourself then your health is affected. You feel exhausted and too fatigued with overwork. You get less sleep and may lose your appetite or may suffer from indigestion. If it happens once in a blue moon then you will not suffer. But if you are in the habit of keeping your work pending then you will surely suffer in the long run. That will take a toll on your health and mind.

Again if you do not have a regular pattern of lifestyle like eating on time and restricting yourself to timely meals and breakfast then your health will be not be affected. Rather your health will remain absolutely sound. Consumption of healthy food is essential to keep your body fit and fine. The tendency to thrive on junk food or oversleeping or not following a routine with regard to sleep and food hampers your health. All these affect your health. Eating healthy food is absolutely essential to remain in sound health. Balanced diet gives us nutrition and we remain energetic and get strength to withstand any physical pressure.

Good diet with the right amount of nutrition is advisable. When you stay healthy your mind too remains alert and you do not feel weak. A person who is robust is found to be cheerful in disposition. Ill health makes one indisposed and incapable of exhibiting energy and zest in work and play.

Health and mind reflect our personality. Regularity and discipline in relation to health and habits provide us with stamina and that develops our mind. Along with that our personality too develops. Eating timely is not everything though. What we eat, the amount we consume and other considerations are there. We need to pay attention to that too. Again we need to have some control over the things that we consume for addiction, like alcohol, smoking and the like. Excessive consumption of alcohol or tobacco is detrimental to health. In a state of intoxication one is likely to lose mental balance and that spells danger as it creates an unhealthy ambience at home. Peace that makes for a healthy surrounding gets affected and gradually it creates disputes and commotion.

So we need to observe restraint and control over our dietary habits. Proper and healthy diet keeps us in good health and mind. Regular exercise keeps us physically fit and in shape. That also helps in keeping our mind alert and sound. Mental exercise revolves round all kinds of intellectual work. Apart from reading one can indulge in games that call for mental exercise like chess, and puzzles that involve numerical solutions. The option is ours. As we feel comfortable we can select our ways and means to stay healthy and sound.

PUNCTUALITY AND PRACTICE

Punctuality is one of the areas of soft skills. Many of you are an expert in your domain where you work with skill and expertise. Yet when it comes to punctuality some of you may have shortfalls on account of that. You may not be punctual with your time and commitment. That is what makes you unpopular among people who otherwise may respect you for your work. So you need to be punctual. Doing your work on time suggests your sense of punctuality. When you are given an appointment it is expected that you arrive for the appointment on time. That shows your punctuality. But if you arrive late and then you go on with your explanation for being late that never puts you in good profile. However expert and sound you may be in your domain your work in totality will always count as your final output. Punctuality too ought to be practised and observed by you to help you in your career growth. If you are punctual then nobody can find fault with you. Whatever you do with expertise and with excellence, needs to be done punctually.

When you reach office you need to be careful about the time. The late comers are always noted. This sends a very repulsive idea about him. Imagine the situation in a slightly different way. You have patient in the hospital passing through a critical stage. The doctor said he would arrive at a certain time. But he is never punctual. He often comes late. And since he has not been contacted he comes rather late that day too. In the mean time the patient's condition worsens and he dies. If the doctor had been punctual then perhaps the patient might have survived. In this case you feel the pinch because you bear the brunt. Had it been just the reverse possibly you would not have felt the intensity of the outcome.

People admire you and respect you if you are punctual. Punctuality helps you in doing things on time. If you are punctual you have no reason to worry on account of being late for any work. If you are punctual you never miss your train or flight. If you are going in a group to some distant place and you are supposed to meet the group in the midway you should be punctual. This is applicable for everyone in the group. If one is late the others suffer. The one who is not punctual exposes himself or herself in the most negative way. So to develop your personality you remember to be punctual always in whatever you do in life.

In the class a teacher scolds her students for coming late. To begin with she excuses two of them. Later she finds one of them has changed and has become punctual. The other however remains the same entering the classroom after five minutes the class begins. The teacher has to tell the student to stay away as she feels disturbed. She cannot spare a student when it becomes a regular practice to come late. He does not grow any sense of punctuality.

When you become a person holding a responsible post in an organization you will see that you cannot tolerate anyone without punctuality. You feel angry if one happens to be unpunctual in any matter. Suppose you are convening a meeting with some of the officials and the first thing that you do is to announce the time. And you see everybody arrives exactly at the time given by you. And if you are not there others will wait for you. Though you are the boss it will be expected that you also arrive on time and come to the venue right at the dot. However sometimes it may be you are held up by an equally important job like in the above case it may so happen that you had a meeting with an important client prior to this meeting. You cannot help it. And it will be understood and appreciated by the others. But if you repeat this practice then your colleagues will have an ill notion of you.

Punctuality is praised and taken up as a quality among great and renowned artists. You must have seen in a show when an artist arrives late how the spectators or the audience get agitated and react. The reason is the late arrival of the artist. May be this is a stance taken up by the artist to keep their audience waiting patiently for them. But that is a very wrong attitude when perceived from the audience's angle.

One imbibes punctuality from the cultural practice that one sees. Unfortunately Indians have been tagged as unpunctual elsewhere in the world. We must endeavour in every way to shed this negative colour so that we earn respect as a person who is very punctual and on time wherever we are.

Whatever you **practise** you acquire dexterity in that. Punctuality is one side of the coin and practice is the other. To achieve outstanding feat in any work you do you need practice. The practice should be done punctually and regularly. You are a golfer. If you aspire to become a national champion in the game you need to practise. That practice has to be done regularly and punctually. If you are to reach the golf course at seven every morning you should be there every day right at seven o'clock without fail. That is what punctuality is. And you practice hard.

A singer has to practise every day and that too punctually. The singer's competence and skill will enhance if he/she sings and practises regularly at a fixed time. Without practice he or she will not be able to retain his/her standard and competence. A swimmer needs to practise swimming every day whether it is summer or winter. Without having regular practice he cannot maintain his dexterity and acumen that he/she may have achieved after a long struggle with it. Moreover in order to reach that height he/she has to practise regularly. And even after reaching an excellent standard in any art or profession one needs practice and assiduous cultivation for reaching further goals. We need to practise writing to develop our writing skills. So we see practice and punctuality help us in not only bettering our worth in any sphere, it also helps us to retain and maintain our standard satisfactorily and excellently.

MOTIVATION

Motivation is a quality that helps us achieve all that we dream of. You want to become a journalist. Your friends and close relatives may give you some brilliant ideas and pictures about the profession and you decide to take up this profession. But one thing is certain. If you want to become a journalist then you must have your motivation from within. Great persons and great achievers have always been motivated by their desire, will and the result of their hard work. If you have dreams, that should motivate you to go ahead. Your motivation should not be an idle one. It should inspire you to work hard. You want to be a journalist because you have been motivated by the truth that you can explore and present through media to the people. You feel the truth must be known by all and you are motivated by the fact that being a journalist you will always be able to present the truth of any happening all around by publishing it. Accordingly you set your goal and work hard to become a journalist.

Motivation provides you with an impetus to work. Whatever you do if you are motivated you can accomplish the job successfully. Motivation is required for attaining the goal. You set your goal but motivation helps you to work for it.

In organizations motivations come in the form of rewards and recognitions. An employee is motivated to deliver his optimum so that organizational goal is reached. Motivations help one to work hard. So as a team leader you need to motivate people in the organization by praising and focusing on their good performance. Speaking openly about someone's good or excellent performance or good effort will help a person to get motivated.

If you feel demotivated while at work try to recapitulate some rewarding moments that will motivate you to work. Depression, frustration and disappointment from any perspective demotivate us. We feel demoralized and cannot perform according to the preset target. That is why it is absolutely imperative for us to find ways that can keep us motivated and also we as leaders, parents or teachers must try to foster the right spirit to motivate all.

Do the same for others as well. Spread goodwill to others not only to motivate to work only but also to motivate to lead a peaceful life.

Leaders are often good motivators. They themselves are motivated to reach their goals and objectives. They also motivate others in the group to reach the same. Motivation involves some key factors. To motivate a person to do something you have to arouse interest in that person in the work for which you want to motivate him. So the initial stage of motivation is to instill the spirit of interest in the person. Once the interest is developed the motivator can direct the person towards the goal. Even the reward for the job itself acts as a motivator. If I do something I desire to get something in turn. That can be in the form of tangible outcome or it can be just recognition of the hard work we do. Whatever it is, it sets the motivation in us. We feel happy to get some kind of reward for the work we do. That reward can be the source of motivation for us.

As friends and well-wishers we can motivate others to indulge in good work. Often we find people are not willing to continue the work they have been doing when they face any shattering situation at home or in the family. It may be a demise, a sad situation or frustration on account of some material loss. Whatever be the condition as well-wisher we can ensure that somebody's good work is continued and it does not stop. For that motivation is required and we must try to motivate that person. That helps him in two ways. He gets engrossed in his work that helps him to overcome his present state of sorrow and discomfort. Besides the work he has been doing is also completed. The ultimate completion of the task also helps in the fulfilment of his desire that perhaps would have remained unfulfilled had there been no proper motivation for him to work.

Incentives and fringe benefits in an organization are tailored to motivate employees. For reaching each targeted goal employees are given incentives so that they are motivated to work with zeal and enthusiasm. Moreover all kinds of entertainment resources are aimed to motivate workers. Everyone on the earth needs motivation to work. A writer's motivation comes from the published work that brings applauses. An artist's motivation comes from the praises and encomium that he/she receives. A scientist is motivated by his thirst for knowing the unknown and following knowledge like a 'sinking star'. An entrepreneur may be motivated by wealth and riches that is the outcome of his enterprise. A doctor is motivated by the nobility of the profession that he has.

The saints and sages of all times are motivated by the heavenly idea of being delivered from this material world in search for ultimate truth of life. Motivation factors are not the same for everyone. It varies from individual to individual. Much depends on the nature of work that calls for motivation.

Challenging situations can be a source of motivation. If one is faced with a challenging situation where one's competence or ability is challenged then it might motivate the person to act with energy and enthusiasm.

Negative reinforcement can also be a source of motivation. If one is given a low ranking for his performance and the concerned person feels that is not a correct evaluation for his performance then it might act as a motivating factor to incite him to work and prove that his worth.

Motivation helps a nation to achieve great success. If we go through the history of any nation we find the cardinal role played by motivation to win a war or overthrow a despotic government. All the great upheavals in history that we read about have been the result of motivated force working from behind.

That is why leaders are known everywhere as great motivators since they possess the quality of charging and igniting people with true potentials to work for a great and noble cause. Motivation is required to develop ourselves and to become a person with the virtues that make us accomplished.

INTEREST AND DESIRE

'I do not have any interest in science'. 'I have lots of interest in film scripting'. 'I would like to be DJ. I am so much interested in this. But you see my dad wants me to join an MBA programme and he is so desirous of my becoming a marketing executive in a multinational company'. What do these comments suggest? They are an evidence of imposition of one's interest on others. The parents' desire pertaining to some areas is forced on a child where the child has absolute lack of interest and desire. In the above cases we see the father's desires are overshadowing that of the son's. They prove that interest lies at the core of our liking and desires and where there is no interest there is a dearth of desires.

Interest shows where we have a liking for. Your interest provides you with motivation. The above comments are mostly the ones we are familiar with. We get to hear similar kinds of comments among our friends. It points out that often parents' desires are imposed upon the children without the consideration whether the children have any interest on that or not. This happens with the adults as well.

Sometimes we feel less interest in the job we do. Just consider the following case. May be by default I have taken up a job seeing the advertised post and the offer promised. After the successful round of interview I find that I have been offered the post. I join thrilled at the prospect of receiving a handsome compensation. After a few days I dislike going to the office. I cannot perform well and deliver the required output. My performance appraisal rating goes down. All these happen because I am not interested in the job I am doing.

It is commonplace that to remain satisfied and happy we should pursue what interests us. And our interest generates the desire to accomplish our task successfully. That is why it is absolutely essential for you to choose the profession you have interest in. Unnecessary imposition of parental desire often results in trauma and disappointment. To evade that problem it is wise to find out from the person concerned the area of his or her interest.

Many among us cherish the illusory notion that if one studies science and technology one will be known as very intelligent. Being influenced by this idea parents often induce their children to opt for science without realizing the fact that they may not have any interest in the subject. This may prove to be a bane since interest motivates us and inspires us to work hard for achieving our goal. Obviously if we pressurize one to do something that one has no interest in then one will not work with zest and neglect and avoid the subject. The consequence will be the student will grow a mental block. He will not show the desired progress and he may fail in the subsequent performances.

Desires come from the interest one has. Whoever is interested in mathematics and counting, desires to study science and technology. The desire is obvious as the person is keen on solving mathematical problems. One who is interested in music since childhood will naturally be inclined towards music and will dream of becoming a musician or a music composer. One who is very keen on painting would dream and desire to become a great artist. If one is allowed to pursue one's field of interest one will perform well and achieve success in life.

You must have seen either on the silver screen or in real life how keen interest and desire leads to the flowering of outstanding achievement from an unexpected corner. To be more precise we have many examples of excellent achievement either in the academics or in the field of creative and performing arts where the individual belongs to parents who have no literacy, poor and humble, situated in a remote part of an undeveloped rural area. This was possible only because there was tremendous interest and desire in the individual that helped him to overcome all barriers and lack of opportunities to get his desired vision realized. He may have worked hard but to begin with it was his interest that grew his desire and that was coupled by his perseverance and aptitude that bore fruit in such an astonishing way.

Whatever desire one has stemming from interest in certain activities in life, one should be allowed to do so. But may be parental wish or societal pressure would not allow him to be what he has inclination for. He may have entirely different interest and perhaps he will be dissuaded to change his views. That is why what happens in several cases is that a child's inclination and desires are neglected and the parental wish and interest is imposed upon. That curbs the personality of the child. The child may not be able to excel as much in the areas where it is forced, as it would have in the area where lay its natural inclination, interest and desire.

As an adult we need to ensure that the child gets the opportunity to do what really interests it. That is how we can help develop a child's interest. That in turn will help it to grow with the right values because it will never suffer from any kind of malice or ill feeling for anyone or anything. To help develop a healthy mind a child should be encouraged to develop its areas of interest. That invariably helps it to perform well in the work it takes up since interest develops the desire to reach the targeted goal. The desire stemming from interest provides an innate urge to work with enthusiasm and full eagerness. That helps one overcome any amount of discomfort one may face in order to do well. If we ensure that children do their work with interest and willingness then we will find less of frustration and disappointment among these children when they grow up to be adults. In fact desires mostly are accompanied by interest and that is why we ought not to direct one's interest to something where one does not have any desire.

Even for the teenagers when they are able to discover their own interests in life it is advisable to counsel and find out their areas of interest and if possible to extend adequate facilities to enable them to develop those inclinations to reach their goal. And this way we can help develop their personalities, talent and potentials to flower in their inherent skills. They will thus contribute to the development of their institutes and nation. Society plays a cardinal role in determining interest in an individual. The age-old concept that certain works are meant for boys definitely proves wrong when by exception some female counterpart happens to achieve outstanding success in performing that job. So to stigmatize specific areas of interest on the basis of gender bias only curbs the growth of a person.

Their contribution will also help the society, country and world to better it in many respects. The flowering of talents in this way will help in the contribution to the welfare of mankind as a whole.

TOLERANCE

Tolerance makes you a respectable person anywhere you go. You need to have tolerance where you find people are incorrigible. Tolerance helps you to get rid of ill-feelings that you cherish against others. If you have tolerance you do not get angry or react easily at one jibing at you. Your tolerance makes you ignore any untoward remark directed to you by others. Tolerance in fact empowers us with cool passivity that is a quality one longs for. Whatever professions you may be in you have to tolerate sometimes things that you may not have thought of. Even in family or close friends and relatives you may have to be tolerant with so many things and situations. Especially with children you need to be tolerant of some of the waywardness they show outside the house. If you tell them anything in front of others then they will develop some traits that may be unacceptable later on in life. Even with spouses and children they may be intolerant.

Tolerance is good and rectification for any intolerable behaviour can be done through counselling and suggestions. Even if the child is small and not capable of understanding then also be tolerant and try to mould the child into disciplinary actions. Moreover if you are tolerant then that will set a very good example and the child will also not repeat its actions.

In any place you go it is wise of you to show your tolerance if you see some misunderstanding taking place between you and the persons you are with. Let us begin from our college days. Sometimes it so happens we find it is difficult for us to tolerate some mischief and pranks played by our friends. When they bully us we fume and fret. And that pleases them. If we get ragged they will be amused and do that more to irritate us. Quite on the other hand if we show our tolerance we outwit them and they stop their pranks on us. Many of our rivalries and disputes take place on account of intolerance.

We show a greater dimension of our personality when we demonstrate our tolerance for other's cultural values, views, perceptions and religions. When you have a broad vision you perceive things from different angles. Your tolerance helps you to respect the values upheld by others, their customs, practices and religious beliefs as well. And that earns you respect and love from people belonging to different communities and religious groups.

Tolerance is a good virtue that we need to cultivate. But surely when things become extremely intolerant then we need to take up some methods of correction. We also need to tolerate various other things in life that we cannot change.

The extremes of climate can become intolerable. But what can we do if we are situated in such a position? We may be in a climate where it is very hot and during the summer it becomes unbearable. We perspire and feel thirsty. Because of extreme heat we are robbed of our energy and may not feel like doing the usual work that we need to do. Yet to adjust ourselves to different situations we need tolerance and in such a situation where we face extremes of climate we need to tolerate rather than expressing discontent at every moment that many of us do. Doing that never solves our problem.

Rather if we tolerate things that we cannot change we feel better. Adjustment and accommodation to various situations and circumstances depends on our power of tolerance. If we have it then we benefit and remain satisfied and seldom suffer on account of such situations.

Suppose you have been raised in the southern part of India where you belong to a family that leads a life of austerity. You are accustomed to the climatic condition of the place, the food habit that you grow in such an ambience. After the completion of your studies you go to Singapore as a hired professional in a reputed corporation. Here you find drastic change in atmospheric condition. Food, climate and lifestyle of the people are so different that you find it difficult to bear. Yet for the sake of the prestigious position that you hold you cannot leave the place and come back to your native place. What you need now is tolerance. If you have tolerance then you do not suffer. You will find lots of intolerable things and situations becoming tolerable with the gradual acceptance of it with the power to tolerate. It is in fact your ability to tolerate that helps you to get rid of the problem cropping up from situations that apparently appear to you extremely intolerable.

In the workplace we come across comments that are intolerable. If it is a downward flow of communication then you feel the pinch but you are helpless as there is hardly any scope for you to interact directly. Moreover to exhibit your reaction may not be desirable. Hence it is prudent of you to be tolerant and accept everything without expressing any negative feeling. You will discover that it paves the way for a better and peaceful life.

Often as parent you face a situation with your kid that simply turns out to be intolerant. But if you tolerate the situation and try to face it with forbearance that may take a different shape and things or situation may improve rather than deteriorate. All over the world we have lots of incidents related to juvenile delinquency and if we explore and probe into the cases we find the majority of them have their roots in an intolerant behaviour from someone concerned. Either it is the parent or some dear ones who had been intolerant and that germinated severe disorder among them. The break-up or split of any close relationship is generally the result of intolerance. All outrageous behaviour results from intolerance. One needs to practise tolerance to develop one's mind healthily. Tolerance gives peace not only to the soul but to others as well. So we need to show tolerance to establish and maintain good relationship with everyone in this world.

Sometimes it may so happen that we have to deal with an intolerant person regularly. In that case we should get accustomed to the person who never shows tolerance with anyone. There is no point in reacting negatively to the person who is not capable of showing tolerance. Even in families we may have someone who is like that. And we have to be in interaction always with such a person. In fact his intolerance makes himself an intolerant person to others. When a person behaves intolerably we should try to find out the reason why he or she does so. There may be psychological setback. There may be some problem related to the person's life. It may be some kind of failure or disappointment that has shattered him or her. In that case he or she may not be very normal in behaviour. He or she may appear intolerable at times. What one would do in such a situation is that one should make use of sanity and normal behaviour and should empathize and try to understand the situation. They should show their tolerance to that person. That would help both. That person with so much of intolerance will realize the positive aspects of tolerance and will perhaps change himself gradually. He will learn to cultivate the habit of tolerating others even when they appear hateful and disgusting.

Tolerance is one of the greatest virtues that can be cultivated by men. We need tolerance for our betterment. When we tolerate others' mistakes it is not that we encourage it. It is a pointer to the one perpetrating the offence. The person realizes his mistakes if he/she has keen sense to understand. That is the best way to correct rather than being too direct and harsh by adopting the means of correction.

Tolerance gives peace to our inner self. We do not lose anything by being tolerant. We benefit by being tolerant. Many among us are endowed with great qualities. But many among those may not have tolerance. Those few must try to cultivate and practise tolerance so that it helps them grow as great personalities.

Religious scriptures teach us to be tolerant. Tolerance helps develop bonding and close relationship. Intolerance creates discord and disharmony without sufficient cause. From a minuscule operation to a large territorial expansion survival and destruction depend on tolerance and intolerance.

HONESTY AND INTEGRITY

Honesty prevents us from all kinds of deception, theft or falsehood that are practised by some in this world. When we talk of ethics the first thing that comes to our mind is honesty. When one is honest one can be depended upon for all kinds of confidential work. An honest person can never steal, cheat or deceive whatever the situation or circumstances he may confront.

An honest person does his work without any falsity or deception. The morals that are indoctrinated in us right from our childhood prevent us from perpetrating offences that make us culpable of any such dishonesty.

However even then many among us do not recourse to truthfulness and honesty despite the morals that were perhaps inculcated in us. Honesty makes us healthy citizens. An honest person can never get involved in deception and treachery. The integrity that we find among the citizens and countrymen comes from honesty and high morals that they uphold. Hence integrity to an organization is one thing that is respected among employees.

There is honesty and integrity involved in professional world. Honest professionals maintain loyalty to the employer and the organization. They are committed to their organization and retain their integrity to the world. The foremost thing that we remember while talking about integrity is that an honest professional does not divulge the confidential matters of his organization even if there is a crisis. Organizations that maintain top secrets related to their functionality and administration need only honest employees who are trustworthy.

An honest person does not misappropriate funds and money that belongs to an organization. He never steals or involves himself in any unauthorized and illegal venture that flouts the norm laid down by the government or any organization. You never find an honest person doing anything unlawful. Even when there is ample opportunity to do something that cannot be spotted an honest person will refrain from doing it. That is what honesty is.

An honest person is respected because he can be given any confidential work. We know there are people who can never be dishonest whatever the circumstances are. A boy who is honest will never compromise his honesty for his own pleasure or amusement. Often it happens that teenagers who find it unacceptable to conform to the restrictions imposed upon them, have recourse to dishonest means to do what they desire.

And they start being dishonest to the parents when they are questioned about their movements and activities. Gradually they practise dishonesty with their teachers, friends and the rest of them. Dishonesty leads one to series of lies as it is very difficult to cover up one lie by another.

Only honest people are able to retain their integrity to an institute or people who they work for. Healthy citizens of the country who have loyalty and integrity remain truthful and honest to their country till the last. History tells us about soldiers, who sacrifice their lives and uphold their loyalty and integrity to their country even at the cost of a very painful and agonizing end.

We know about the stalwart personalities who are known for their honesty and integrity. Honest people are the pride of their families and nation. Honesty and integrity in the professional world is essential. Teachers who are honest never adopt any unjust means to win favour among the students. A teacher may set the question paper but her honesty prevents her from revealing the confidential work that she has been engaged at.

Honesty makes people sincere and truthful. They are all interlinked. That is why telling lies or hiding the truth to remain on the safe side ought to be discouraged right from the beginning. Childhood is the stage when this needs to be instilled in children. Parents and teachers should themselves adopt honesty and practise it to set examples.

Nations are known for their goodness and nobility. If corruption and crime rate are high in any country then it reflects that people are not very honest. Dishonesty may be among some people in every country. But what is important is whether dishonesty prevails in greater magnitude or not. This has a social bearing as well. If in an organization ninety per cent of the people are honest then one per cent will feel discouraged and hesitant to do anything dishonest. It is like social influence. Whatever be my inclination that becomes negated if I see good examples all the time. I may have a tendency to be dishonest but if I am circled around with people who are all honest then I will have an influence on me that may gradually change my values and outlook.

Honest citizens of a country can make their country a place of pride where a foreigner will not feel hesitant to move about freely. It will be inspiring for any foreign national to learn to be honest and retain one's integrity likewise.

Honesty makes our home a happy place. The spouses need to be happy and trust each other to keep their commitment. Any treachery or dishonesty ruins the bond that is built on mutual trust, honesty and integrity. Children get examples from their parents. They should see examples of honesty right in front of them to grow up to be individuals with such morals that will endow them with a commendable personality.

HUMILITY

Humility is an ornament that is a source of inspiration to everyone in this world. Humility gives us the nobility to respect and regard our friends and others with courtesy and decorum. A humble person is respected by all. It is more so when one is an achiever. Imagine someone is very successful and has won acclaim for his/her outstanding achievements. But you do not find any trace of arrogance or pride in his/her behaviour and interaction with others. Neither does he/she show any vanity or feeling of superiority. What will be your feelings and impressions about him? You will respect him for his humility. That is what humility is.

Your personality is further developed and you are admired when you are humble and modest.

You find your boss who has recently joined very bright and is known for his brilliant academic career. He has excellent career graph and he is young and dynamic. He is the youngest Managing Director of your company. Everybody in the office is under the impression that he is unapproachable because he is so bright. May be he will brook no nonsense. This keeps you away from him and you feel that he must be very proud and conscious of his achievement and position.

But ultimately when you meet him you find he is totally different. He is so humble that he does not hesitate to call you in an endearing term and address you so politely. Immediately he becomes your favourite and he holds a place of respect in everybody's heart because of his humility. People who are not modest are not easily liked by others. Pride makes one unpopular. Whatever be one's achievement if one is proud and haughty then nobody likes to socialize with him or her. Humility makes one noble and the gestures of humility are remembered by people.

Humility does not imply you bow down to everybody and do not walk boldly or talk with confidence and assertion. Quite on the other hand humility gives you the strength to be bold and courageous to give your honest opinion and views to others.

Whatever achievements we have in life we do not need to show off. We can be noted by others even if we remain humble. Rather our humility will evince good spirit and wishes in all. That is most obvious when we cite examples. Shri is a student who has graduated from one of the best colleges in the town and he happens to have topped the university. When this student interacts with others he does it with politeness and modesty. His interaction with his teachers is remarkable.

Everybody speaks highly of him. That is because of his good nature and humility. Though he happens to be the topper he is the humblest of all the students in his class. There are other students who are arrogant and try to display their skills in communication by speaking English and by trying to adopt false accents purposely to glorify their skill. Ironically this group of students is much below in standard when it comes to studies or communication skill. Rather Shri is the one who commands respect and admiration from others because of his humility. He is the best in ability and competence and he is the most humble of all. He could have been proud and too conscious of his ability. Yet he remains modest that is manifested in his interaction with his elders and classmates. This is an example of humility that adorns the personality of an individual.

We have our legendary tales that bear the examples of how an unassuming and modest person ultimately wins respect and love from everyone. There are stories in Aesop's Fables where we have tales that tell us how humility wins over pride and arrogance.

The stark contrast in personality traits can be noted in this regard when we juxtapose a nouveau-riche with a wealthy aristocratic individual. Those who have seen wealth and riches for many generations do not generally boast of wealth and riches. They wear a garb of humility as wealth does not seem to them anything remarkable they have seen and have enjoyed. But those who may have made wealth recently and have experienced the pleasures of life generally have a tendency to boast of their riches and wealth. They are the ones who seem sham in front of the modest persons who have humility even if they stand out as very rich and wealthy.

LOVE AND FAITH

Love is an oft used expression that has wide connotations. It implies a relationship that exists among human beings. Human relationship entails intricacies that are difficult to define. We all are subjected to whims and fancies that mainly are governed by our passion and feelings of love. We have love for so many people in this world. When we talk of love we emphasize mainly on the relationship existing between two individuals belonging to opposite sex. From there it grows into a bond of family and then the strong ties we have in the relationship between the mother and child, between parents and children, between the siblings, between grandparents and grandchildren and so on. Love is used synonymously to express affection. We talk about a teacher's affection for her students. Someone's affection for children or an uncle's affection for his nephew or niece stems from love. Actually there is a subtle difference between all these feelings. But at the core there is involved emotion.

Love is one of the basic components of human emotions. We can never think of an individual without love. There is a saying that a man devoid of love is capable of killing any one on the earth. It is unthinkable that anyone can be without this common human emotion that has its manifestations in so many ways. Sometimes there can be variations in proportions. All of us like a person who is capable of loving others. Hence people with love and affection are liked by others. Mothers are an epitome of love. Mother's love for her children is supposed to be selfless. Mothers dedicate their lives for their kids.

Love makes our personality admirable. Selfless love for mankind is philanthropy. There are people who are known for their philanthropy and they are held in high esteem. Children also grow up to be loving and caring when they are taught to love others. When they become adults they realize the value of being loved and considerate to others. Love is not restricted and confined to only human beings. We also learn to love our country, our environment and even the animals that reside the earth. So this feeling is pervading in so many ways in human beings.

We also love God. The feeling is different. All of us do not believe in God. Naturally this feeling is not shared by all. But some devotees are there who have profound love for God. Their love is rooted in faith. Love and faith are interdependent as we perceive in human relations too.

Without faith you cannot have true feelings of love. The bond that is built of love also gives faith. We know that we have faith on those people we love. We cannot doubt a person's integrity or loyalty where we have genuine feelings of love.

Love can be the cause of various feuds and they result in all kinds of discord. But if one is governed by the feeling of sincere and honest love one never causes harm to others. That is always reflected in the personality and they are the persons to influence and impact others by their love.

Let us explore how love can make our personality impressive and admirable. In our interaction with anyone belonging to the world of profession we go by certain protocols demanded in the world of profession we work. There the tender feeling of love may not have much importance, but at least what we require is love for our work. And that gives us the success we dream of. Of course our skill and competence is required but on top of it we need to have love for our work and that will develop our interest and desire. Once we opt for a profession in life we need to grow not only liking for the job but love for the work as well. That is how we get love and appreciation for our work from our boss too. Our good work in turn earns us love and respect from others in the organization.

Among friends and relatives we spread goodwill and love. It is love that binds us together, whether it is friendship or relationship existing in the family. The eldest member in the family has lots of responsibility and he fulfils his commitment to the members of his/her family with love, sense of duty and responsibility.

His love forbids everyone in the family to refrain from doing anything that he does not like. Of course for that he has to uphold some principles in life. He should exhibit those qualities that make him respectable as an elder in the family. He must cultivate patience, tolerance and courage to remain honest whatever be the situation. That is how he can get love and respect from all the family members.

All religions teach us to love and care for others. Love governed by selfishness and motivation does not make anyone happy and peaceful. It may become difficult at times to be absolutely unselfish when we love another being. We can take examples. Two friends love each other. They always help each other when required. Yet there is an underlying selfishness in their relationship. What makes it amazing is that nobody understands that from outside. It is only when a crisis takes place that the truth comes out and the relationship gets a jolt. What is important here is to understand that genuine feelings and unselfish attitude helps one to attain that good relationship existing between two persons having unselfish and genuine feelings of mutual trust and love. Otherwise relationship thriving on selfish motivation can never be long lasting and easily destroys the intimacy called friendship.

All these qualities or personality traits that we have been discussing so far help us to grow our sense of values and ethics. When we talk of values we mean the ability to discriminate between good and bad and value what is correct and good from life's perspective. With these discrimination grows our ethical sense. We develop our personality by adhering to morals and values that are respected in society.

Literature helps us to have a vision and changed perception. But when we practise in reality what we think should be done do we actually benefit out of it.

I go by examples that help us to get a clear vision of the whole thing. A college student has his examination round the corner. He does not study at all. He watches movies, chats with his friends, goes to gym and freaks around wasting his time. When ultimately the examination knocks at the door he is in a soup. He does not know a single thing about his subject matter. He then manages to write his paper by cheating and adopting unique methods of unfair means. All these he does by racking his brain to devise various means of cheating the authorities and also himself. For, he remains ignorant and does not know anything that he is supposed to know. One may cheat others but at the same time one cheats oneself, by depriving him/her of the knowledge he/she would have had, had one studied and taken the examination in the right way. Examination is a yardstick to evaluate one's knowledge and merit in the subject. If we cheat do we get the right perspective of the evaluated parameters that reflect our merit and knowledge level? It is also making us unethical and immoral. Today I cheat my examiner and I develop myself as a cheat. Who is the person benefitting? My examiner remains what he was but I remain an ignorant fool.

Thus if one adopts unfair means right from this age one is likely to grow unethical values later on. That will hamper his personality. He will not hesitate to do anything unfair and unjust in later life as well. When this same person is hired as an employer he will without scruple adopt all kinds of dishonest means for his personal gains and career benefits and will not try to work hard for career growth.

A person who is dishonest is never respected by others whatever his achievements in life may be. Dishonesty never makes a person happy. If anyone adopts dishonest means to get something in life then one remains in constant apprehension for being discovered. That robs him of peace and happiness that an honest person enjoys.

Good moral values help you to lead a life of satisfaction and complacency. One who is governed by sound sense of ethics has always a clear conscience that gives him joy and peace. He remains absolutely free from any unnecessary worries. A person with right moral values never feels the temptation to get something that is not due to him. Right values guide him to live an honourable life and have a respectable place in society.

The morals we imbibe are passed on to the next generation. The behaviour, personality and perceptions of an individual are reflection of the morals and values he has received from his parents. Parental responsibilities are paramount in making their children grow up with right values and morals. The values like honesty, truthfulness, loyalty and integrity can be there in an individual if he grows up in a healthy environment at home with parents upholding high morals and values.

Individual values are affected if one is in a bad companion and ignoble society. That is why it is essential to be in good society right from childhood so that we grow up to be good noble citizens.

Conclusion

'Personality Development' comprehensively involves two perspectives. One is how personality develops with the defined traits. And the other is how personality can be developed by fine-tuning these traits in us. In fact if we try we can develop our personality in the desired way. I have discussed detailing the areas where one can focus on to develop one's personality. However at the conclusion I would like to focus on another aspect of personality development. Read the following:

'She's caring, supportive and all that a grandchild would wish for in a grandmother. That's my loving *ajji,* who is stepping into her 100th year now. An extremely warm person, she knows life like nobody else. Married at a young age, she lost her first son and her husband in quick succession early in life. She was left to face a bleak future with a small baby (my dad). But, not one to give up on life easily, *ajji* took to farming and brought up her son single-handedly.'

The article published in Soul Curry in the supplement of *Sunday Times of India,* November 13, 2011 is where Mala Viswanath talks about her grandmother who braved all oddities with her grit and determination. This is an example that enables us to realize the harsh realities that few of us face. From their tales of struggle and odyssey we perceive the magnitude of the personalities of those people.

I have till the previous chapter, focused on those areas that help develop our emotional quotient. My endeavour has been to demonstrate how you can improve your emotional balance so that you can shape your personality that everybody respects and reveres. When we talk about emotional intelligence we can take examples from such personalities like the one I have quoted from Soul Curry featuring in the *Times of India*.

The inner self is very important in the sense you acquire peace and stability of your mind. In this digital era when life is taking a shape of a robot, it is difficult for one to breathe and sigh comfortably. We are continuously goaded by aspirations, spiralling desires and hunger for power. The unending desires to reach one goal after another keeps one always on one's toes. There is hardly any opportunity for an individual to devote to pleasurable pursuits. Even if one goes for a pleasure trip one is likely to receive calls to be reminded of an important errand. And in this mechanism our existence seemingly operates nowadays. In the midst of all these we have to live and live like a human being with all the elements of tranquillity of mind.

Urbanization has lent us physical comfort. But it has robbed us of peace of mind. We know there are limitations in everything. So we need to think prudently and with a sound sense of discretion we must determine the better ways to live healthily. Instead of being vulnerable to the limitations of the urban reality we can hone our soft skills so that we can lead a peaceful life.

There has been an awakening all over the world for spiritual uplift. This book is not meant for spiritual guidance. What it wants to bring home to you is the fact that in the throes of fast, digitized and competitive world we can develop ourselves into beings with personalities that will provide examples to the others and create a place in the heart of every soul. We need to remember that a noble person is one who by his personality impresses every one. How does he do it? He does it by the deeds that speak of his behaviour, conduct and manners all considered to be the reflection of his personalities. That is why it is essential for you to develop your personality so that you can set an example and create an iconic image that will captivate the people of the world. It is not necessary that you have to do great deeds that will make you be remembered by everyone around you. If you are a person with a charismatic personality with a sound sense of etiquette, manners, goodwill upholding values and principles that are respected in the cutting edge of technology then you will be admired and liked by all. And you will be happy and satisfied too. All of us aspire to be known, liked and respected by others. Many of us do get that. Many of us do not get it. The reason is the ones who do not get are those who need to brush up those skills that enhance and sharpen the required elements for developing their personality.

You focus on those elements that comprise the key features of personality. Developing personality does not mean to be smart and talk well and dominate over others. Personality development implies overall growth and elevation of thinking process as well. When you think well you will automatically be inspired to talk well and do your work well. That will raise you tomorrow much above from the level that you are in today.

All our deeds are executed being dictated by our mind that is the source of our thinking process. The way to think correctly comes from different levels of perception. It is not always that we perceive everything correctly at one go. Our perception keeps changing with time and experience. But once we gradually learn to think and develop our inner perception by training and controlling our mind through concentration and meditation we will find our thinking perspective has changed.

Our personality will change and become better once we are governed by our spiritual intelligence. Spiritual intelligence does not refer to sitting in one place and chant mantras in front of the idol that we believe in. It is totally a different view in the sense you develop your mind through your deep realization and understanding the futility of worries and anxieties that engulf us. Our emotional intelligence will take a leap forward when we develop ourselves through spiritual intelligence.

Let us discuss in detail what precisely we mean when we talk about spiritual intelligence. Spiritual intelligence is the intelligence that we acquire through meditation and through the realization of ultimate truth pertaining to the goal and purpose of life.

What is the goal and purpose of life?

To live happily we may acquire all the comforts and physical pleasures that apparently seem to give us happiness. Still we may be looking for something more that will make us happy from within. The search goes on. We try to reach that state when our mind will get freedom from the earthly concerns in life. We look longingly for peace and absolute rest from all physical and mental pressures that we go through. Some of us face various situations when life's patience is tested. And in such a predicament it seems to those people how to come out of such a situation. There are degrees of sufferance endured by people. In extreme sufferance people experience such intense agony that they are the ones who look for a relief of their burdened soul in the form of heavenly bliss. They crave for the respite that only their still and serene mind laden with pure thoughts without any temptations from within can provide them. It is that state that is the ultimate purpose and goal of life.

When we reach such a state that we know the joy of life's fulfillment. It is then that our souls and not the body only, experience the heavenly bliss that even the richest holiday resort in the world cannot give. That explains why people even after getting the desired object that they crave for like success in work, academic achievement, material comforts, riches, name and fame yearn for something more. And that something more is provided by spiritual intelligence when people realize that there is something beyond the physical comforts that we look for. That is the key to our bliss and happiness to stay with a mind filled with completion. The purpose of life is to attain peace of mind when we experience bliss in the true sense of the term.

Spiritual intelligence does not prompt you to abstain from the comforts that you have got and give up all the pleasures of a comfortable living and lead life of austerity and hardship. It is absolutely your choice what kind of life you lead. It is not that you have been blessed with fortune and success that you have to repudiate them and lead a life of a sage to get spiritual intelligence. It is not at all so. Spiritual intelligence helps you to attain that wisdom that provides you with peace and serenity of mind in the midst of all the worries, anxieties and troubles you may have to face. We cannot give up our job, our responsibilities or our duties pertaining to life that we live. The concern here is the emptiness and void that we feel at times even after obtaining all the desired objects that we sought in life. It is at that point of life that we finally seek that ultimate truth that is an eye-opener. When we realize that cosmic truth then we are a changed personality, who believes in accepting things as they come in life.

This world of technology and fast developed civilization has enabled us to learn so many things. It has procured the means of comfort and safety. Think of the medical sciences and the benefit man is reaping from the advances made by it. For any disease that one suffers one can easily take medical advice and becomes well after being cured by the doctor. From the point of view of the patients it is a boon since the advanced medical science has made diagnosis process more accurate and precise as it is more technology based in the current time. This is possible because of the inventions and advent of electronic devices and machines. The steady progress of medical science has made the job of the physicians and surgeons error free and less cumbersome. Technology by its gadgets and telecommunication system has enabled the rapid progress in the field and we reap the benefit out of it. Medical science has now become instrumental in man's staying healthier and living longer.

Yes we live longer and the present generation enjoys the fruit of the rapid progress made by medical science. Now for any ailment we run to the doctor for consultation, diagnosis and cure. And we feel sure that we will receive the best of treatment if we go to the doctor specializing in the areas that need medical care and treatment. If we spend according to the requirement then we are sure to get the patient treated and cured. There is the feeling that everything will go well and we go by that assumption. The chances are there that in any ailment if proper care and medication is given then the patient suffering from the ailment will get cured. However there can be exceptions when despite the best of treatment the patient may succumb to death. What do we do in such cases? We feel sad and miserable and find it difficult to accept the hard reality. But we have to. After all that is an inevitable fact that science and technology cannot stop.

We see there are many things in life that cannot be brought under control by man. We have achieved so much and we are trying to explore and advance further. The endless endeavour to live a better life is there in human beings. And we will not stop. But this exploration of material world will not be sufficient for us to live a life of calm and peacefulness. We need to explore the world that will give us comfort of mind as well. The anxiety, worries and the endless urge to go further and further make us fatigued mentally. It is then that we yearn for the bliss that is associated with the calmness of mind. This yearning is evoked in our mind at one point or the other. Thousands of people all over the world are suffering from depression, anxiety, nervous disorder and other symptomatic diseases. The origin of those symptoms is the present living that we have. In order to come out from this shell of constant and persistent threats that enslave us we need to develop our mind and personality. We need space to satisfy our mind's desire of peace and contentment. We need peace and absolute tranquillity.

To achieve that, we should develop our mind. The mind and person go together. We think and try to reach the goal. The positivity of mind is imperative. If we try we can achieve whatever we need to develop our personality. Only thing is that we must have a positive outlook to accomplish the not- so- impossible a task. The first positive step to develop our personality is to begin setting examples to our younger generation. If we are emotionally stable and behave in a stable manner even in crises and troublesome situations we will set examples for the others to follow.

As parents or teachers we need to develop our personalities in such a way that our children or students will have those parameters required for them to grow into good and honest persons. Children imitate and get influenced by their parents. So parents have a contributory role to play. The parents must set noble examples of honesty and righteousness. That is absolutely essential. Things that appear to us not so important may assume a formidable shape later on in our life. Children have the power to observe and they cannot be neglected. Treat a child in the way you would while you deal with an adult. Children are sensitive. They have the natural tendency to emulate and copy what they observe among the adults.

The following points are very important for all of you to remember.

- Be truthful and try to avoid resorting to falsehood. If you are simple and do not get affected by outward forces you can retain your simplicity. And that will also help you in developing emotional balance and emotional intelligence.
- Be punctual. This goes especially for teachers who have the responsibility to pave the right path in front of the students whose personality is shaped according to what they see. Students are not matured enough to decide what is wrong and where they make mistakes. Everything is easy to say but it is equally difficult to practise entirely. A person who is matured and has developed his personality can explain everything clearly and patiently. Patience is required for the teachers to interact with students. So as a teacher your responsibility is to talk to your students patiently without being affected by their waywardness. That will help the students to be persons with patience and be in the habit of talking patiently with everyone they come across.
- Be bold and confident. There are people who have the potentials to do great deeds. But they often retract because of fear of struggle and hardship.

There are various circumstances and situations when you feel absolutely helpless. At that time you may not have anyone so close in whom you can confide and give vent to your feelings. You feel like talking to someone, may be a very good friend of yours. But he or she may be thousands of miles away from you. In crisis or in a sad state of mind you really do not know how to cope up with your situation. You feel disorganized and your mind is restlessly wandering into the mazes of anxiety and sadness. Who is to show you compassion and comfort?

Many will answer: 'Why don't you visit the social networking site and meet your friend to exchange your pleasantries? That will give you comfort and rest.' But is not that very mechanical approach to life? Do you really get the comfort that your scalding soul is looking for? What you require then is absolute peace and rest. You can get it if you train your mind. At home you can select your comfortable place sit and stay quietly freeing your mind from the agony and pain that have been troubling you.

The wealthy and the rich all over the world have incredible comfort to make them happy. They have lots to provide them with satisfaction and contentment in life. If you consider fame they have it. If you consider wealth they have it. When you think of their happiness it is very difficult to pronounce the right word that is associated with their happiness. The wealth and glory may have made them happy. Yet if asked they may say that they need something more. This is the desire they have. Desire with limitations is fine but when anyone is obsessed by it to get more and more then it becomes intimidating. It is a universal truth that one cannot get everything in life. Somewhere or other they find something is lacking. That is the want they suffer from and often it assumes a gnawing pain. Growing wealthy, famous or known is fine when perceived from a distance.

They appear to be the happiest beings on the earth. Yet when you take a closer look you discover their desire and hankering after more and more keep them always at pain and worry. Deep down within them is a submerged feeling of dissatisfaction and provoking craze to get more and more. That creates the unrest and instability of mind.

Let us talk of people belonging to ordinary walk of life. Your life begins with your career that you need to traverse. May be you go through lots of trials and tribulations and you achieve success. You feel happy at the success you have got. You begin your career as a management trainee. Two years later you become the manager of a branch office. After the tenure of five years you are promoted to the regional office as an in-charge. Gradually by the time you are fifty you become one of the top notches. You are initially very happy but it is some kind of provocation that works and you feel like having more. Now you are having what most people in your place would have got. Yet there is a subdued desire to get more and more. That gives you no rest. The constant setting of goals is the thrust that we have. To some extent it is good to have those goals. But when it becomes unbounded and takes you on and on creating an illusory world like a mirage you feel the sudden jolt at one point. The mind travels so fast that it does not reach a satiating point. The body becomes worn out and there is a conflict of mind and body taking place. To come out from this we need space enough for the mind to rest.

Apart from the professionals or employees working for organizations, we have scores of entrepreneurs. An entrepreneur begins with one venture. He or she works for raising and making it prosperous. He/she works hard with enthusiasm and face obstructions perhaps in several places. After all nothing in life is a smooth sail. The hardship that the entrepreneur goes though teaches him patience, courage and tenacity. But there is no certainty that he will be successful in his venture. He may fail miserably where he may have to suffer a great loss both financially and resource wise. What does he do at that time? Few can remain stable during such failure.

Again it can be the reverse. You begin a venture and become very successful in doing that. What can be your next step? You have dreams of setting up a second venture and then you set up another. Now you have dreams that goad you to embark on project after project. You never foresee the risks that you take in investing lump sum of money for a series of projects. This again entails ambitions and high hopes of getting name, wealth and fame. After all successful projects will bring you fame as well.

The above cases cite instances of emotional responses one goes through when one confronts similar situations. Not that all of us are successful in our ventures though. Some of us may face rather awkward situations. We may fail in our enterprises. The reasons may be any.

How can it affect a person is our concern here. We get frustrated in such circumstances and do not know how to cope up with such a situation. May be we have incurred huge monetary losses and feel crestfallen and miserable. However we cannot back out as that will result in further loss. So to keep up our patience at that time is imperative. To chalk out a strategy is important. Listening to the experienced ones and taking advice from the successful persons in similar venture is also needed. To do all these, presence of emotional intelligence is a must.

In the family, we find mothers get rather tensed with the children's achievement. It can have two types. Either the mothers are too happy with the progress of the child or it can be they are overambitious and expect more and more from their children. Here a tremendous psychological pressure works.

The mothers who have not been successful in their lives and who have not been able to achieve what they dreamt of, try to see in their children the dream come true potential. So they express the desire in many cases in an uncannily abnormal way. This is the modern day's pressure that children face.

Not only in academics there are other areas where the parents put undue pressure in the minds of their children. Parents should realize the potentials their children have and accordingly they must advance and proceed. The problem in the present era is tough competition among people. We turn ourselves into machines always involved in competition and vying for the coveted place in society.

This is detrimental for the growth and development of personality. Healthy competition is good. But the moment we start comparing our child's ability with that of another we create the germs of petty jealousies and meanness not only in our mind but in our children also who will grow up with these inhibitions and that will ultimately shatter their mind and peaceful living.

There is no end to personal desire that human beings cherish. Those desires keep them dream high end goals achieving some of which may be next to impossible. Those dreams that remain unfulfilled are transmitted to the posterity. The pressure is built for the next generation too. They are set with targets to reach or obtain which again there will be the same amount of struggle. If one achieves it is fine. When there is a story of a failure then the repetition of the transmission of 'dream fulfilment desire' takes place. This goes on. To come away from this a strong personality is required. If you are not strong then you will be vulnerable to all kinds of false egocentric problems like these. Your children who are future citizens of the country will develop traits of fear psychosis, insecurity and doubts while doing anything.

Freedom is desirable for the development of personality. The feeling of freedom in thoughts and plans literally makes one enthusiastic about doing something challenging in life. Freedom in respect to movements also gives one the courage and spirit to work and think independently. For developing personality we all need freedom of thought and action.

How far that freedom can be extended is a different issue. Freedom does not limit oneself to boundaries. When we consider freedom that has no gender bias we obviously see in that certain serious issues. They are with respect to freedom of teenagers. Teenagers get freedom for their activities and growth. They need to have freedom of choice of studies, careers, marriage and also some decisional roles in the family. Yet societal values differ from country to country. In Indian context we can assert that there is a margin drawn while giving freedom to our children and teenagers.

Freedom for girls and boys does not assume the same import in social context. Freedom of girls during the teenage may demand limitations. However that depends on the circumstantial requirement and parental outlook. But freedom in thoughts and intellect are absolutely necessary for the growth and development of inner self of an individual. Regarding this we need to remember that a nation can grow prosperous where there is no gender bias and where equal freedom is extended to both male and female members of an institute and organization.

In this context I must discuss the gender based discrimination made in some of the communities in our country. We still have some families or communities who give importance to the male child and make some discriminatory decisions in some important aspects of life. For example, a girl child is not allowed to pursue higher study rather she is married in accordance with social norms. The same does not apply in case of a male child. Disregarding the capabilities or other factors a boy in those communities is encouraged to pursue his desired career. The discrimination leaves behind an impact on the personality development of an individual. A girl is deprived of the opportunities that make her feel diffident perhaps and later on it affects her personality. The independence, that is curbed at her childhood of thinking and dreaming of her future ultimately affects and shapes her personality development.

People holding responsible posts need to ensure the implementation of equality and freedom to all irrespective of gender, caste and community. Then only can a nation grow to acquire excellence in all spheres. It is seen that there has been continuous revamping of organizational stance with regard to human resource development. The leadership trends and human resource optimization have received a radical change in the current age. The immense possibility of talent development is deeply related to personality development of an employee. How can personality reflect the potentials of a human being? The answer is that when a person is given freedom and independence to use his competence and inner strength to prove his worth he/she is more at ease to accomplish a goal. The departmental heads are assigned responsible position to do their job. But if the person is not allowed freedom in thoughts and expressions then his/her contribution will be marred as it would deprive him/her from taking initiative in doing anything out of the box that may ultimately be beneficial to the organization. That will affect the organizational development as well as the career growth of the individual.

The old and retired ones suffer from sentimental blocks created by loneliness and debilitating faculties. They too need developed personalities so that they could have spent their old days in peace and harmony. We find old people all over the world feel alienated and lead a lonely life.

This problem that besets the aged ones is a common one. My only suggestion to them is that they should not feel they are unwanted. The old people seek comfort in an old-age home. But that is not always possible. Wherever one is, one can think of spending time in occupying oneself in mental exercises like reading or teaching or any such activities that give them joy. That is a very good source of deriving joy. Gardening keeps an old person happy because in the process of growth and blossoming of a tree or a plant the old one can have a symbolic vision of regeneration. The grandchildren that the old has can be thus an inspiration and motivation to live.

Today's youth will become tomorrow's old. They must develop their personality in such a way so that they can become emotionally intelligent and spiritually alert to be able to accept life as it comes. Change is bound to occur. When there is a collapse of an age old system or when there is a radical change in any sphere then the ones who are emotionally intelligent are able to face it with contentment and stay unaffected.

The problems that beset human beings can reach their extreme levels. It is the emotional intelligence that makes one withstand the unassailable misery and plight that may come in life sometimes assuming a formidable shape. When we stand in a hopeless situation we need to confront it with calm acceptance. Unalterable situations make us patient, courageous and submissive. That develops our mind and perception so that we learn to sympathize with others' predicament. In fact the more trials and tribulations one faces in life one becomes stronger and bolder to confront any challenging situation. That is how one's personality develops.

Personality development has various stages. But prime importance that childhood has cannot be ignored.

Childhood is the stage when subtle feelings and interactions leave behind a mark in the mind. That influences the personality of an individual as he develops.

In conclusion I would like to say that human beings are fallible. They need to correct time and again to find out what could be the best way to live. If we develop our personality in the way I have discussed I feel we will have peace and happiness in the hi-tech era where we get physical comforts in opulence but we seek peace and stability of mind.

Personality development is imperative not only for the professionals who need to thrive in the corporate culture. It is imperative for the ordinary people too. All of us need to be endowed with good personality so that our goodness and nobility become an inspiring source for others. Down the ages we have witnessed people with outstanding personalities who have been remembered for their extraordinary deeds in the world. They are wonders to us as they are the epitome of virtues we desire to be endowed with.